The Art of Governance: Leadership, Strategy, and Vision for Global Influencers

By Ali Raza

Preface

Leadership has always been a cornerstone of human progress. From ancient civilizations to the modern world, societies have looked to their leaders for guidance, vision, and inspiration. Yet, the challenges of leadership today are unprecedented in their complexity and scale. Climate change threatens our planet, economic disparities deepen social divides, technological advancements outpace ethical considerations, and political polarization erodes trust in institutions. At this crossroads, the call for transformative leadership has never been louder. This book, *The Art of Governance: Leadership, Strategy, and Vision for Global Influencers,* seeks to answer that call.

Leadership is no longer the purview of a select few. It transcends political offices and corporate boardrooms, extending to activists, educators, entrepreneurs, and community leaders. In this interconnected world, where individual actions ripple across borders and generations, leadership is about more than personal ambition or short-term success. It is about building systems, fostering collaboration, and creating a legacy of equity and progress. This book is an invitation to leaders from all walks of life to embrace the art of governance and wield their influence with purpose and integrity.

Why This Book Matters Now

We live in an era defined by paradox. On one hand, globalization, technology, and innovation have unlocked possibilities unimaginable just a few decades ago. On the other hand, these same forces have amplified disparities, fueled conflicts, and strained the planet's resources. The speed and scale of change leave little room for complacency. Leaders today must navigate a world where the stakes are higher, the margins for error slimmer, and the consequences of inaction more severe than ever before.

Amid these challenges lies immense opportunity. The crises we face—whether environmental, social, or political—are also catalysts for transformation. With bold vision and ethical governance, leaders can turn division into dialogue, stagnation into innovation, and despair into hope. But this requires a new kind of leadership: one that prioritizes sustainability over expediency, inclusivity over exclusion, and legacy over immediate gratification.

This book was written to equip leaders with the mindset, tools, and strategies to meet this moment. It offers a comprehensive framework for leadership that blends historical lessons, philosophical insights, and actionable guidance. From fostering ethical decision-making to building enduring alliances, from transforming ideas into movements to leaving a legacy that inspires generations, each chapter addresses a critical dimension of governance. Together, these elements form a blueprint for leadership that is both principled and pragmatic.

The Foundations of the Book

At the heart of this book lies a simple but profound idea: leadership is both an art and a science. It requires creativity and discipline, vision and strategy, empathy and resilience. Great leaders are not born—they are forged through reflection, learning, and purposeful action. This book draws on timeless principles while addressing the unique challenges of the 21st century. It is as much a guide for self-improvement as it is a roadmap for societal transformation.

Each chapter delves into a key facet of leadership:

1. **The Nature of Governance:** Leadership is compared to the art of crafting, requiring patience, precision, and adaptability. This foundational chapter explores the balance between tradition and progress, freedom and responsibility, and individuality and unity.
2. **Accountability and Proportionality:** Governance thrives on fairness and trust. Leaders must build systems that promote accountability and balance competing priorities to ensure equity and sustainability.
3. **The Power of Ideas:** Ideas are the seeds of change, but their true potential lies in their implementation. This chapter examines how leaders can cultivate and champion ideas that foster collaboration, innovation, and progress.
4. **Ethics in Leadership:** In a polarized world, ethical leadership is a moral and practical imperative. Leaders must prioritize integrity, transparency, and empathy to bridge divides and rebuild trust.
5. **Sustainability and Resource Management:** Effective governance depends on the responsible stewardship of resources. This chapter emphasizes the importance of balancing economic development with environmental conservation and social equity.
6. **Transforming Ideas into Movements:** Ideas ignite change, but movements sustain it. This chapter provides a framework for mobilizing people, building alliances, and maintaining momentum to drive systemic change.
7. **Building Alliances:** No leader succeeds alone. Alliances rooted in mutual respect, shared goals, and equitable benefits are essential for addressing global challenges.
8. **Leaving a Legacy:** The final chapter explores what it means to lead with the future in mind. A leader's legacy is defined not by personal accolades but by the systems, values, and progress they leave behind.

Leadership Beyond Titles

Leadership, as envisioned in this book, is not confined to titles or positions of power. It is a mindset and a commitment to driving positive change, regardless of one's sphere of influence. A teacher shaping the minds of future generations, an activist fighting for justice, a CEO transforming their industry with ethical practices—all are leaders in their own right. This book celebrates this diversity of leadership and seeks to empower individuals across domains to harness their potential.

At its core, this book is about people. The ultimate measure of leadership is not the wealth accumulated or the monuments built, but the lives improved and the opportunities created.

Effective governance is about serving humanity, ensuring that the systems we build today pave the way for a brighter, more equitable tomorrow.

Historical Inspiration

The principles in this book are enriched by the examples of leaders who have left enduring legacies. Figures like Nelson Mandela, Mahatma Gandhi, Franklin D. Roosevelt, and Angela Merkel illustrate what it means to lead with vision, integrity, and resilience. Their stories remind us that leadership is not about perfection but about persistence and purpose. They teach us that lasting change is possible when leaders align their actions with their values and inspire others to do the same.

Modern Challenges, Timeless Lessons

The challenges of our era—climate change, social inequality, political polarization—may seem unique, but they are part of a continuum of human struggles. The lessons of history provide invaluable guidance for navigating these challenges. From the Dust Bowl of the 1930s to the civil rights movement, from the rise of democratic ideals to the fight for sustainability, humanity has repeatedly demonstrated its capacity for resilience and reinvention. This book draws on these lessons, offering leaders the tools to turn obstacles into opportunities.

An Invitation to Reflection

Leadership is deeply personal. It begins with self-awareness and a willingness to reflect on one's values, motivations, and goals. This book encourages leaders to ask themselves:

- What values define my leadership?
- How do my decisions impact the people and systems around me?
- Am I prioritizing short-term gains or long-term progress?
- What legacy do I wish to leave behind?

These questions are not just rhetorical—they are a compass for navigating the complexities of governance. Leaders who embrace this reflective approach are better equipped to act with clarity, conviction, and compassion.

A Call to Action

This book is not just a theoretical exploration—it is a call to action. The world needs leaders who can rise above division, inspire trust, and take decisive action with courage and integrity. It needs leaders who are unafraid to challenge the status quo, who value collaboration over competition, and who prioritize the collective good over personal ambition. This book seeks to empower such leaders, equipping them with the insights and strategies needed to create meaningful and lasting change.

Leadership is not easy, nor is it always rewarding in the moment. But it is one of the most profound and impactful pursuits a person can undertake. Leaders have the power to shape the future, to build systems that uplift, and to inspire others to reach their full potential. This book is a guide for those who are ready to embrace that responsibility.

The Journey Ahead

As you journey through the chapters of this book, you will encounter a blend of historical wisdom, philosophical insights, and practical frameworks. You will be challenged to think critically about your role as a leader and inspired to take bold steps toward progress. Whether you are a seasoned leader or an aspiring one, this book offers something valuable: a roadmap for governance that is ethical, visionary, and transformative.

Leadership is not about the power you wield but about the impact you create. It is about the ripples you leave in the lives of others and the systems you strengthen for future generations. The art of governance is a lifelong journey, and this book is your companion on that path.

The challenges we face are immense, but so is the potential for change. Together, we can build a future defined by equity, progress, and hope.

Welcome to the art of governance. The world needs your leadership.

Introduction: The Call for Transformative Leadership

The modern era is defined by its complexity and interconnectedness. Climate change, geopolitical upheavals, widening economic inequality, and the rise of societal polarization create a landscape fraught with challenges but ripe with opportunities. These global dynamics demand a level of leadership that transcends traditional approaches. Leaders today must possess not only the ability to address immediate crises but also the vision to anticipate and shape a sustainable future.

Leadership, once perceived as the domain of elected officials and statesmen, now permeates every corner of society. CEOs of multinational corporations, grassroots organizers, social influencers with millions of followers, and heads of international institutions share a common mantle of responsibility. They must act as stewards of progress and architects of solutions in an increasingly fragile world.

This exploration of governance is a call to action. It challenges leaders to see their roles as more than operational managers. Instead, they must embrace their capacity to inspire, innovate, and elevate those they serve. Anchored in history, informed by philosophy, and driven by pragmatic strategies, this vision of governance offers a transformative path forward.

Part 1: Leadership as an Art—Morality, Vision, and Empathy

1. The Moral Compass of Leadership

Leadership begins with a foundation of moral integrity. History teaches that leaders who lack a strong ethical grounding may achieve temporary success but ultimately fail to inspire trust and long-term loyalty. From Mahatma Gandhi's principles of nonviolence to Nelson Mandela's emphasis on reconciliation, moral leadership is the cornerstone of enduring influence.

A leader's moral compass must guide decisions, ensuring that personal gain or expediency does not overshadow the greater good. This principle is especially critical in today's polarized environment, where ethical lapses can result in public backlash, eroded trust, and societal disillusionment.

2. Vision: Seeing Beyond the Immediate

Vision distinguishes true leaders from mere managers. While managers focus on executing tasks and maintaining the status quo, leaders see the big picture, envisioning a future that others might deem unattainable. Visionary leaders possess a unique ability to identify emerging trends, harness opportunities, and rally their teams toward collective goals.

For example, during the height of the U.S. civil rights movement, Martin Luther King Jr.'s vision of equality resonated deeply because it painted a picture of a future worth striving for. In the corporate world, leaders like Elon Musk challenge conventional norms by envisioning the possibility of multi-planetary habitation. Such vision inspires action, turning challenges into stepping stones for progress.

3. Empathy and sensitivity: The Bridge Between Leaders and Followers

Empathy is the glue that binds leaders to the people they serve. Without understanding the hopes, fears, and aspirations of their constituencies, leaders risk becoming disconnected. Empathy allows leaders to craft policies and strategies that resonate on a human level, making them relatable and effective.

nse of freedom is central to societal harmony, enabling coordination, cooperation, and velopment. Civil liberties are essential because freedom allows individuals to speak freely, fostering growth and progress. Different types of freedom are listed:

1. Freedom of religion and belief.
2. Freedom of expression.
3. Freedom to adopt any career.
4. Freedom of movement.
5. Freedom to marry and divorce.
6. Freedom to hold and dispose of property.
7. Freedom to receive education.
8. Freedom of association.

The absence of such freedoms leads to societal stagnation, as observed in communist nations, which the text compares to prisons. Freedom increases productivity and enriches society, creating opportunities for ideas to flourish. This sustains life and prosperity. Nature itself thrives on balance and pulsation, and human society mirrors this.

Consider New Zealand Prime Minister Jacinda Ardern's empathetic leadership during crises such as the Christchurch mosque shootings and the COVID-19 pandemic. Her ability to connect emotionally with her citizens fostered trust, even amidst difficult circumstances.

Part 2: Strategy as a Science—Pragmatism, Adaptability, and Innovation

1. Pragmatism: Grounding Vision in Reality

While vision provides direction, strategy ensures execution. Pragmatism in governance requires an acute awareness of available resources, constraints, and risks. Leaders must strike a delicate balance between ambition and feasibility.

Pragmatic leaders excel at aligning long-term goals with immediate actions. This approach was exemplified by Franklin D. Roosevelt during the Great Depression. His New Deal policies showcased a blend of bold vision and practical steps to address unemployment, economic instability, and social unrest.

2. Adaptability: Thriving in Uncertainty

The speed of change in today's world demands adaptability. Technological advancements, shifting public sentiment, and global crises necessitate that leaders remain flexible, recalibrating strategies as circumstances evolve. Rigid adherence to outdated methods can spell disaster in a rapidly changing environment.

The COVID-19 pandemic highlighted the value of adaptable leadership. Organizations and governments that pivoted swiftly—embracing remote work, accelerating digital transformation, and reshaping healthcare delivery—emerged stronger. Leaders must cultivate this ability to navigate uncertainty while staying anchored to their core mission.

3. Innovation: Driving Progress Through Creativity

Governance is as much about breaking new ground as it is about preserving stability. Innovation lies at the heart of solving today's most pressing challenges. Leaders must foster cultures of creativity, empowering teams to think beyond traditional paradigms.

Take the example of Satya Nadella's leadership at Microsoft. By championing innovation and a growth mindset, he transformed the company's culture, leading to breakthroughs in cloud computing and artificial intelligence. Leaders who prioritize innovation can unlock potential that transcends conventional limitations.

Part 3: Governance in Action—Equity, Sustainability, and Global Collaboration

1. Equity: Building Inclusive Systems

Governance must prioritize equity to ensure that leadership benefits all segments of society. Economic disparities and social injustices can erode the foundations of stability, leading to unrest and disillusionment. Leaders must champion inclusivity, designing systems that uplift marginalized communities and bridge divides.

Programs like the Scandinavian welfare model illustrate how governance rooted in equity can create prosperous, harmonious societies. These systems prioritize universal access to education, healthcare, and social support, demonstrating that equity is not only morally right but also strategically advantageous.

2. Sustainability: A Moral and Strategic Imperative

The existential threat of climate change underscores the urgent need for sustainable governance. Leaders must act decisively to balance economic growth with environmental preservation, ensuring that future generations inherit a habitable planet.

This requires bold action, such as the Paris Agreement's commitment to reducing carbon emissions. Sustainability is not merely an environmental issue; it is a cross-cutting priority that impacts global security, public health, and economic resilience.

3. Global Collaboration: Harnessing Collective Strength

No single leader or nation can tackle global challenges alone. Effective governance requires collaboration across borders, sectors, and cultures. Leaders must embrace multilateralism, leveraging international partnerships to address issues like pandemics, cyber threats, and resource scarcity.

The success of global initiatives, such as the eradication of smallpox or the development of COVID-19 vaccines, illustrates the power of collective action. Leaders must prioritize diplomacy and cooperation, recognizing that humanity's greatest achievements are born from unity.

Part 4: Practical Frameworks for Transformative Leadership

1. Systems Thinking: Understanding Interconnectedness

Leaders must approach governance through the lens of systems thinking. This involves recognizing the interconnected nature of global challenges and crafting solutions that address root causes rather than symptoms. For example, tackling poverty requires addressing education, healthcare, and employment simultaneously.

2. Stakeholder Engagement: Building Consensus

Effective governance relies on engaging diverse stakeholders. Leaders must build coalitions that include governments, private enterprises, civil society, and individuals. Consensus-building fosters legitimacy and ensures that solutions are both inclusive and sustainable.

3. Metrics and Accountability: Measuring Success

Transformative leadership demands transparency and accountability. Establishing clear metrics for success allows leaders to track progress, adapt strategies, and maintain public trust. Metrics should encompass economic, social, and environmental dimensions to reflect holistic progress.

Conclusion: Inspiring Greatness in an Era of Complexity

The art of governance is an ever-evolving endeavor that demands a harmonious blend of morality, strategy, and vision. Leaders must be both dreamers and pragmatists, capable of inspiring greatness while navigating the intricacies of modern challenges.

In this age of transformation, leadership is not a title but a responsibility. It is a call to serve humanity with courage, wisdom, and integrity. By embracing the principles outlined in this guide, leaders can rise to the occasion, shaping a future defined by equity, sustainability, and collective progress.

The world is watching. The time for transformative leadership is now.

Chapter 1: The Kiln of Society – A Metaphor for Leadership

Governance, at its core, mirrors the art of crafting—a process that demands patience, precision, and an intuitive understanding of natural laws. The metaphor of a kiln—a tool used for baking bricks—is an evocative framework to understand the dynamics of leadership and society. A kiln's intricate balance of heat, ventilation, and arrangement provides critical lessons for leaders tasked with fostering cohesive, resilient, and progressive societies.

In a kiln, the balance is delicate. Without proper ventilation, the build-up of gases can destroy the bricks. Similarly, societies that lack mechanisms for open dialogue, representation, and innovation risk implosion. Leadership, therefore, is not just about wielding authority but about cultivating conditions where every "brick"—every citizen, community, and institution—can withstand the pressures of time.

The Importance of Ventilation in Leadership

Ventilation is the lifeblood of a kiln, ensuring that heat is evenly distributed and gases escape freely. For societies, this represents the mechanisms through which people express concerns, ideas, and aspirations. Without avenues for free speech, accessible justice, and fair representation, societal pressure mounts to dangerous levels. Leaders who prioritize such "ventilation" ensure stability by addressing grievances before they escalate into crises. Human society requires outlets for grievances, creativity, and expression. The Bible reminds us in **Galatians 6:2**, *"Carry each other's burdens, and in this way, you will fulfill the law of Christ."* When individuals and communities are denied the chance to "ventilate" through free speech, fair governance, or social support, societal tension escalates, potentially leading to conflict or upheaval

Case Study: The Arab Spring – A Lesson in Suppression

The Arab Spring, a wave of uprisings across the Middle East in the early 2010s, underscores the dire consequences of neglecting societal ventilation. Authoritarian regimes across the region suppressed dissent, silenced opposition, and ignored the voices of the marginalized. These conditions led to a build-up of frustration, which eventually erupted into widespread protests.

The uprisings revealed a stark lesson: **delaying or ignoring grievances does not resolve them; it only intensifies the pressure.** In Egypt, for example, decades of political repression and economic stagnation culminated in the ousting of President Hosni Mubarak. Tunisia's revolution sparked regional unrest after Mohamed Bouazizi, a street vendor, set himself on fire in protest of systemic injustices. These movements were a collective cry for dignity, freedom, and equity— fundamental human needs that had long been ignored.

Leadership Takeaway:

- Leaders must proactively address societal grievances through **transparency, inclusivity, and reform**.
- Suppression might delay dissent, but it cannot eliminate it. **Proactive governance**, with mechanisms for open dialogue, is far more effective than reactive crisis management.

Balance and Accountability in Governance

Just as bricks in a kiln must be arranged with precision to ensure uniform exposure to heat, governance requires a careful balance of competing interests. Leaders face constant trade-offs: economic growth versus environmental preservation, individual freedoms versus collective security, and tradition versus innovation. Navigating these tensions requires accountability, fairness, and a commitment to long-term stability over short-term gains.

Case Study: Post-Apartheid South Africa – Balancing Justice and Unity

Few leaders have faced the challenge of balancing societal fractures as profoundly as Nelson Mandela in post-apartheid South Africa. Mandela inherited a country deeply scarred by institutional racism, economic inequality, and mistrust. Yet, rather than succumbing to the pressures of revenge or retribution, Mandela prioritized reconciliation.

Through initiatives like the **Truth and Reconciliation Commission (TRC)**, South Africa confronted its past while building bridges for the future. The TRC allowed victims of apartheid-era abuses to share their stories, while also granting conditional amnesty to perpetrators who confessed. This process, though imperfect, balanced accountability with forgiveness, preventing the country from descending into further conflict.

Leadership Takeaway:

- Leaders must confront past injustices to create lasting peace. Ignoring historical grievances only deepens societal wounds.
- Balancing **justice** with **unity** is critical. Policies must address pain while fostering inclusion and hope.

Practical Strategies for Leaders

The kiln metaphor emphasizes that successful governance is both an art and a science. Leaders must build systems that channel societal energy constructively, ensuring that every individual has the opportunity to contribute to and benefit from collective progress. The following strategies translate this metaphor into actionable practices for modern leadership:

1. Institutionalize Dialogue

Establishing regular, structured avenues for dialogue allows leaders to stay attuned to societal tensions. Public consultations, citizen assemblies, and digital forums can serve as effective tools for engagement.

- **Example:** Finland's citizen panels actively involve residents in policymaking, ensuring their voices shape national priorities.
- **Impact:** Regular dialogue builds trust, defuses frustration, and strengthens democratic legitimacy.

2. Promote Transparency

Transparency fosters trust between leaders and the people they serve. Sharing data, decisions, and progress openly enables citizens to hold leaders accountable while aligning their expectations with reality.

- **Example:** Estonia's e-governance platform allows citizens to access government services and track decision-making processes in real-time.
- **Impact:** Transparency reduces misinformation and empowers citizens with knowledge.

3. Invest in Equity

Systemic imbalances in wealth, education, and resource access are major sources of societal tension. Addressing these disparities not only reduces grievances but also unlocks untapped potential within marginalized communities.

- **Example:** Rwanda's investments in universal healthcare and education have spurred economic growth while reducing inequality.
- **Impact:** Equity-driven policies foster social cohesion and resilience.

Reflection for Leaders

Leaders, like kiln masters, must constantly evaluate the conditions under their stewardship. The following reflective questions can guide their approach:

1. **Are grievances being heard and addressed?**
   - Ignoring discontent can lead to unrest. Leaders must create avenues for feedback and respond with tangible action.
2. **Are policies equitable, or do they favor specific groups?**
   - Uneven policies breed resentment. Equity should be a cornerstone of governance.
3. **Is the system flexible enough to adapt to emerging challenges?**

    o   Rigid systems are vulnerable to collapse. Leaders must embrace adaptability to remain effective.

Societies as Kilns: A Framework for Leadership

The kiln metaphor offers a profound insight: societies, like bricks, need care, balance, and ventilation to endure. Leaders who neglect these principles risk presiding over systems that fracture under pressure. On the other hand, leaders who embrace them foster environments of resilience, innovation, and unity.

Key Insights from the Kiln Metaphor:

- **Ventilation (Expression):** Societies need mechanisms for open dialogue and innovation to thrive.
- **Heat (Pressure):** Pressure, if managed constructively, strengthens societal bonds and drives progress.
- **Balance (Accountability):** Leaders must carefully weigh competing interests to ensure long-term stability.

Through this lens, governance transcends the mere exercise of authority. It becomes an art—an intricate craft requiring foresight, empathy, and a relentless commitment to the greater good.

Conclusion: Leadership as a Kiln Master

The kiln of society is an evocative metaphor that illuminates the intricate dance of leadership. Just as a skilled kiln master oversees the baking of bricks, adjusting the heat, ventilation, and arrangement to ensure durability, leaders must cultivate societal conditions that enable resilience and progress.

In today's complex world, the stakes are higher than ever. Inequality, climate change, and geopolitical tensions demand leaders who are both artisans and strategists. By embracing the principles of ventilation, balance, and accountability, they can shape societies that withstand the pressures of time and evolve into models of equity and innovation.

Leadership, like crafting, is not a one-time effort. It requires constant care, adjustment, and reflection. The kiln metaphor serves as both a cautionary tale and a source of inspiration, reminding leaders that their legacy is built not only on what they achieve but on the foundations they lay for future generations.

Chapter 2: Balance and Dichotomy – The Roots of Stability

"Equilibrium is the essence of life, and governance is its custodian."

In nature, balance is achieved through pairs of equal and opposite forces. This principle is evident in human anatomy, where the left and right sides of the body mirror each other, maintaining equilibrium. Similarly, societal structures thrive on balance. Male and female, positive and negative, right and left—all are inherent dichotomies that contribute to the stability of human life and organization.

The interplay of these directions is critical for societal harmony. Consider the family unit: the roles of men and women, though different, complement each other to create a balanced and functional whole. Beyond families, the same principle applies to larger social groupings—tribes, nations, and belief systems. Diversity within these groups, though it may appear to create tension, is what sustains a healthy and adaptive society.

As stated in **Ecclesiastes 4:9-10**, *"Two are better than one because they have a good return for their labor. If either of them falls, one can help the other up."* This scripture underscores the importance of balance and mutual support,

Human existence thrives on balance, a delicate and intricate interplay between opposing forces. Light and darkness, tradition and progress, individuality and unity—these dichotomies define the rhythm of life. While they may appear contradictory, they are, in truth, complementary. When managed wisely, they create harmony and fuel growth. In governance, the art of maintaining balance between these tensions is the foundation of stability, resilience, and advancement.

The role of a leader is not to suppress or eliminate these tensions but to embrace and channel them, weaving disparate forces into a cohesive and dynamic whole. Leadership, like life itself, is an ongoing dance between opposing but interdependent elements. This chapter delves into the importance of balance in governance, examining historical examples, philosophical insights, and practical strategies to equip leaders with the tools they need to foster stability in an ever-changing world.

The Dichotomies of Governance

Governance exists at the crossroads of competing forces. Effective leaders must recognize, respect, and manage these dichotomies to ensure the prosperity and adaptability of the societies they serve. Understanding and navigating these opposing forces allows leaders to build dynamic systems capable of enduring the pressures of modern governance.

1. Tradition vs. Innovation

Tradition anchors societies, providing a sense of identity, continuity, and stability. At the same time, innovation drives progress, adaptation, and relevance. The challenge for leaders lies in honoring cultural heritage while embracing forward-looking change.

Case Study: Japan – A Harmonious Balance

Japan exemplifies the delicate balancing act between tradition and innovation. On one hand, its society treasures rituals like tea ceremonies, festivals, and traditional arts, ensuring that its rich cultural heritage thrives. On the other, Japan is a global leader in cutting-edge technology, from robotics to sustainable energy solutions. This dual commitment has not only preserved its unique cultural identity but also positioned Japan as an economic and technological powerhouse.

Key Insight for Leaders:

- Respect for tradition fosters social cohesion and cultural continuity.
- Openness to innovation ensures a society remains competitive, relevant, and prepared for the future.
- Leaders must create policies that both protect cultural heritage and promote technological and social advancements.

---

2. Individuality vs. Unity

Individuality celebrates personal freedom, creativity, and self-expression. Unity emphasizes collective purpose, harmony, and social cohesion. Societies that lean too heavily toward one side risk fragmentation or suppression. Successful governance requires a nuanced approach that values individual expression while fostering a sense of shared identity.

Case Study: The European Union – "United in Diversity"

The European Union embodies the principle of balancing individuality and unity. Its motto, *"United in Diversity,"* reflects the bloc's effort to maintain the distinct identities and cultures of its member states while pursuing shared goals of economic and political integration. While tensions arise, the EU's framework allows countries to retain sovereignty while benefiting from collective strength. This balance has contributed to peace and prosperity across a historically divided continent.

Key Insight for Leaders:

- Fostering spaces for individual expression within a unified framework enhances societal harmony and resilience.
- Leaders must promote inclusivity, ensuring that diverse voices are heard while cultivating a shared vision for progress.

3. Freedom vs. Responsibility

Freedom empowers individuals to pursue their aspirations, unleashing creativity, innovation, and ambition. However, unchecked freedom can lead to societal disorder, inequality, and exploitation. Responsibility, on the other hand, ensures that freedom is exercised in ways that promote equity and strengthen the social fabric.

Case Study: Scandinavian Social Models – A Blueprint for Balance

Countries like Sweden and Denmark exemplify how to balance freedom with responsibility. These nations emphasize individual freedoms—such as the right to education, healthcare, and expression—while promoting collective responsibility through high taxes and robust social welfare systems. The result is high standards of living, strong social cohesion, and global leadership in sustainability and equality.

Key Insight for Leaders:

- Freedom and responsibility are interdependent and must be nurtured together.
- Leaders must ensure that individual rights are exercised in ways that contribute to the greater good rather than undermining societal stability.

4. The Impact of Monolithic Societies

In some systems, such as those historically associated with communist ideologies, diversity is often suppressed in favor of a uniform, monolithic structure. These systems aim to eliminate the natural dichotomies and variations that exist in society—erasing distinctions of religion, gender, class, and even regional identity. While this approach may create a surface-level unity, it often leads to deeper fractures.

For example, the Soviet Union attempted to homogenize its vast and diverse population under a single ideological framework. While this strategy brought certain economic and military efficiencies, it also led to the suppression of cultural and regional identities, creating long-term unrest. The collapse of the Soviet Union in the 1990s unleashed decades of latent tensions, as previously suppressed groups sought to reclaim their identities and autonomy.

Similarly, in modern-day examples, countries that attempt to impose rigid uniformity often face internal dissent. For instance, the ongoing challenges in China's Xinjiang region, where cultural and religious homogenization policies have been implemented, reveal the difficulty of maintaining control in a monolithic society.

Philosophical Foundations of Balance

Throughout history, philosophers and spiritual traditions have emphasized the centrality of balance in governance and life. Their insights offer timeless guidance for modern leaders striving to navigate complexity and tension. Balance is a universal principle that governs all aspects of life. From the equilibrium of nature to the checks and balances in governance, maintaining harmony ensures stability and progress.

Mathematical Balance: Just as equations require both sides to be equal, societies need to balance opposing forces, such as innovation and tradition, freedom and responsibility.

Social Balance: A society that values both individuality and unity creates a dynamic environment for growth. For example, multicultural nations like United States thrive by promoting inclusivity while respecting cultural differences

1. Taoism: Harmony in Opposites

The Taoist concept of *Yin and Yang* reflects the balance of opposites. Darkness and light, femininity and masculinity, stillness and motion—these forces sustain the universe through their interplay. Taoism teaches that balance is not static but dynamic, requiring constant adjustment.

2. Aristotle's Golden Mean

Aristotle championed the idea of the *Golden Mean*, the virtue of moderation that lies between extremes. For instance, courage is the balance between recklessness and cowardice, and generosity is the balance between extravagance and stinginess. Governance, similarly, must avoid the pitfalls of excess and deficiency.

3. Biblical Wisdom: Fairness and Equilibrium

Proverbs 11:1 states, *"A false balance is an abomination to the Lord, but a just weight is His delight."* This highlights the moral imperative for fairness and equilibrium in human affairs. Leaders are called to uphold justice by creating systems that are equitable and balanced.

Application for Leaders:

- Governance must embody these principles by valuing balance over dominance.
- Policies should avoid extremes, seeking fairness and moderation to sustain societal harmony.

The Consequences of Imbalance

When balance is neglected, the repercussions are often severe, destabilizing societies and undermining progress.

The forced elimination of natural dichotomies can lead to polarization. In societies where balance is disrupted, people are often pushed into opposing camps. For example, the political landscapes of many nations today reflect a growing divide between "right" and "left," with moderates increasingly sidelined. This polarization is not limited to politics—it extends to gender roles, cultural identities, and even technological debates.

In a balanced society, these dichotomies coexist and complement each other. However, when one side is suppressed or overemphasized, the resulting imbalance leads to friction and instability. The polarization we see in contemporary politics, from the United States to Europe, can often be traced back to an erosion of this balance.

The Bible provides wisdom on this topic in **Proverbs 11:1**, *"A false balance is an abomination to the Lord, but a just weight is His delight."* This speaks to the universal need for fairness and equilibrium, both in individual relationships and broader societal structures. Below are key examples of the dangers of overemphasizing one side of a dichotomy:

1. Economic Inequality

Unchecked capitalism widens the gap between the wealthy and the poor, leading to social unrest and eroding trust in institutions.

- **Example:** The 2008 Global Financial Crisis was fueled by deregulated markets and excessive risk-taking. The resulting economic collapse devastated millions of lives and exposed the dangers of prioritizing profit over equity.

2. Cultural Suppression

Efforts to forcibly homogenize diverse cultures often breed resistance and resentment, destabilizing societies in the process.

- **Example:** China's policies in Xinjiang, aimed at assimilating Uyghur culture, have faced global condemnation and internal unrest. Suppression of cultural identity not only violates human rights but also weakens societal cohesion.

---

3. Political Polarization

Extreme partisanship undermines governance by stalling decision-making and exacerbating divisions.

- **Example:** The United States often experiences political gridlock due to deep ideological divides between parties, delaying critical reforms and eroding public trust in government.

Case Study: Post-Apartheid South Africa – A Masterclass in Balance

Nelson Mandela's leadership in post-apartheid South Africa exemplifies the transformative power of balance. Upon becoming the nation's first Black president, Mandela faced immense challenges: a deeply divided society, demands for justice from the oppressed majority, and fears of retribution among the privileged minority.

Strategies for Balance:

1. **The Truth and Reconciliation Commission (TRC):**
   - This initiative allowed victims of apartheid-era abuses to share their stories and seek justice while granting conditional amnesty to perpetrators who confessed their crimes. The TRC balanced accountability with forgiveness, fostering healing without igniting cycles of vengeance.
2. **Institutional Reform:**
   - Mandela dismantled apartheid-era structures while creating inclusive frameworks for governance, ensuring equal representation and opportunities for all citizens.

Outcome:

South Africa transitioned to democracy without descending into civil war, demonstrating that balance can turn deep divisions into unity.

Frameworks for Balancing Dichotomies

Leaders can employ the following strategies to navigate competing forces and foster equilibrium:

1. Inclusive Policymaking

The preservation of individuality within a framework of collective harmony is the key to societal success. By recognizing and celebrating diversity, societies can achieve sustainable progress. As the Bible teaches in **Proverbs 11:14**, *"For lack of guidance a nation falls, but victory is won through many advisers."* This wisdom reminds us that collaboration, rooted in respect for individual differences, is the foundation of a prosperous and peaceful world

Create platforms where diverse groups can contribute to decisions, ensuring that all voices are heard.

- **Example:** Switzerland's participatory democracy allows citizens to vote directly on key issues, fostering inclusivity and trust.

2. Dynamic Systems

Develop policies that are adaptable to changing circumstances while maintaining core values.

- **Example:** Finland's education system evolves continuously, incorporating new research and innovations while upholding its commitment to equity and excellence.

3. Cultural Preservation Funds

Allocate resources to safeguard cultural traditions, ensuring they coexist with modernization.

- **Example:** UNESCO's efforts to preserve endangered languages underscore the importance of protecting cultural diversity in a globalized world.

4. Principles of Balancing: Universal and Timeless

1. **Natural Pairing:** In nature, things are created in pairs—such as hands, eyes, and even genders. This duality is essential for harmony, as it allows for interdependence and mutual support.

2. **Human Bonds:** Relationships between individuals or groups—whether familial, social, or professional—act as the "glue" of society. These bonds are strengthened by understanding, cooperation, and shared goals.
3. **Governance and Culture:** When societies are governed by rules and traditions that reflect their unique identities and values, they thrive. Respecting cultural differences while promoting universal human rights is key to creating cohesive communities.

These principles can be observed not only in ancient times but also in contemporary societies, where the balance between tradition and modernization often determines stability and growth.

---

5. Grouping and Balancing: Lessons from Nature and History

1. **Interdependence in Nature:** Nature demonstrates the importance of grouping and balancing in countless ways. For instance, ecosystems thrive when all elements—plants, animals, and microorganisms—work together. Similarly, human societies flourish when individuals and groups contribute to the collective good.
2. **The Role of Politics:** Political groupings have long been a means of organizing societies to achieve common objectives. Today, this need is amplified by advances in technology and communication, which bring new challenges and opportunities. For instance, the global response to the COVID-19 pandemic showcased the necessity of coordinated action across nations.
3. **Opposites in Harmony:** The dichotomy of right and left, male and female, positive and negative is inherent in creation. These opposites are not meant to compete but to complement each other, ensuring balance and continuity. For example, modern governance systems often benefit from a balance of conservative and progressive ideologies, each contributing unique perspectives to societal development.

---

6. Avoiding Conflict: The Power of Understanding

While war and violence may seem like inevitable outcomes of human differences, history shows that they are often the result of a failure to balance opposing forces. The Bible teaches in **Matthew 5:9**, *"Blessed are the peacemakers, for they will be called children of God."* This divine wisdom underscores the importance of resolving conflicts through dialogue and mutual understanding.

Wars are often fueled by the suppression of opposing voices. For instance, the Cold War was not only a geopolitical struggle but also a clash of ideologies that left millions of lives disrupted. The lesson here is clear: suppressing diversity leads to conflict, while embracing it fosters peace.

7. Preserving Identity: The Role of Rightists and Leftists

In any society, there are individuals and groups who strive to preserve their unique identities—whether cultural, linguistic, or ideological. These are the "rightists," who value tradition and continuity. Opposing them are the "leftists," who seek to challenge norms and drive progress. Both roles are essential, as they create a dynamic equilibrium that propels society forward.

For example, in the United States, the ongoing debates between conservative and liberal ideologies reflect this natural dichotomy. While conservatives emphasize preserving foundational values, liberals advocate for adaptation and change. Together, these forces ensure that society neither stagnates nor loses its roots.

8. Monolithic Societies and Their Challenges

Communist countries often aim to create monolithic societies by eliminating diversity in governance, culture, and ideology. While this approach may offer short-term stability, it often leads to long-term unrest. Without opposition or alternative viewpoints, these systems can become rigid and oppressive.

For instance, the collapse of the Soviet Union highlighted the unsustainability of such monolithic systems. Similarly, modern examples, such as North Korea, reveal the deep social and economic challenges of suppressing diversity.

9. The Need for Balance in a Polarized World

Today's world is increasingly polarized, with divisions not only between nations but also within them. This polarization is often exacerbated by technology, which amplifies echo chambers and deepens ideological divides. Yet, the solution lies in the timeless wisdom of balance and coexistence.

As we navigate these challenges, we must remember the words of **1 Corinthians 12:14-20**, *"Even so the body is not made up of one part but of many. ... If the whole body were an eye, where would the sense of hearing be? If the whole body were an ear, where would the sense of smell be?"* This metaphor reminds us that diversity is not a weakness but a strength, allowing societies to function as cohesive and adaptive entities.

By embracing this principle, we can move toward a future where harmony prevails over discord, and the collective good is prioritized above individual or group interests.

10. The Role of Balance Between Opposing Forces

The cooperation of opposing ideas—whether through political ideologies, societal movements, or cultural norms—holds immense potential for progress. The coexistence of contrasting views, such as those of rightists and leftists, creates a system of checks and balances that ensures no single ideology dominates, leading to a more nuanced and sustainable path forward. This dynamic interplay has historically been instrumental in societal advancements.

For example, consider the bipartisan system in the United States. While Democrats and Republicans often clash ideologically, their coexistence forces dialogue and compromise, preventing extreme policies and encouraging solutions that address diverse perspectives. Similarly, global institutions like the United Nations rely on the cooperation of ideologically diverse member states to tackle worldwide challenges, from climate change to economic inequality.

11. Ideological Complexity in a Global Context

In the contemporary world, the variety of voices and ideas poses a significant challenge: how can we create systems that allow diverse perspectives to contribute constructively? The answer lies in fostering cooperation and goodwill among those with differing ideologies, recognizing that no single perspective can address the complexities of modern life.

Ideas can generally be categorized into two types: positive and negative. While positive ideas aim to build and improve, negative ideas often seek to dismantle or oppose without offering viable alternatives. A functional society must balance these forces by providing platforms for all voices to be heard, ensuring that positive contributions are maximized while negative tendencies are moderated.

For instance, the European Union exemplifies a framework where nations with different histories, languages, and priorities work together to promote peace and prosperity. While disagreements arise, the EU's foundational principles of cooperation and compromise have allowed it to remain one of the world's most successful supranational entities.

The Concept of Union: A Path to Stability

The idea of union—whether among individuals, groups, or nations—is essential for addressing common challenges and achieving shared goals. Union amplifies the collective strength of its members, enabling them to tackle objectives that would be impossible individually.

1. **Strength in Unity:** A union derives its power from the combined efforts of its members. As an example, consider how threads woven together form a rope capable of lifting immense weights, while a single thread would snap under pressure. Similarly, the strength of the United States lies in its federal structure, which unites diverse states under a common framework.
2. **Preventing Fragmentation:** In regions bordering the former Communist bloc, the absence of unity has often led to fragmentation and instability. The ongoing conflicts in Eastern Europe highlight the dangers of division, as countries struggle to reconcile historical grievances with modern aspirations.
3. **Balancing Individuality and Collectivism:** A successful union respects the individuality of its members while encouraging collaboration. The failure to balance these elements can weaken the union, as seen in the dissolution of the Soviet Union, where the suppression of national identities ultimately led to its collapse.

Unity vs. Unanimity: Understanding the Difference

There is a distinct difference between unity and unanimity in governance. Unity implies collective agreement on overarching goals, while unanimity demands complete conformity. The former is achievable and sustainable, while the latter is an unrealistic expectation that often leads to suppression of dissent.

Communist regimes, for example, have historically strived for unanimity by eliminating opposing voices. However, this has often resulted in long-term instability and eventual collapse, as seen in the disintegration of the Soviet Union. In contrast, democratic systems thrive on unity in diversity, where differing perspectives coexist within a framework of shared principles.

Alliances and Balance in International Relations

Forming alliances among nations or parties is one of the most effective strategies for maintaining balance and achieving peace. However, alliances must be rooted in mutual benefit and clear objectives. Without clarity, alliances can lead to exploitation, as more powerful entities often dominate their weaker counterparts.

For example, NATO has successfully operated as an alliance based on shared security concerns and mutual defense. Its effectiveness lies in its clear guidelines and collective decision-making processes. On the other hand, alliances formed on imbalanced terms—such as certain colonial arrangements—have historically led to resentment and eventual uprisings.

Virtue and Vice in Leadership and Society

The coexistence of virtue and vice is an intrinsic part of human existence. Societies and individuals must actively work to ensure that virtue remains dominant. This is achieved through ethical governance, education, and community engagement.

The metaphor of a coin with two sides—one representing virtue and the other vice—captures this duality. Just as flipping a coin reveals either side, circumstances and leadership decisions determine whether virtue or vice predominates. A society that prioritizes virtue creates conditions for justice, peace, and prosperity. For instance, post-apartheid South Africa prioritized truth and reconciliation, enabling the country to move forward despite its painful past.

The Upsetting Effect: When Balance is Disrupted

The "upsetting effect" occurs when societal balance is disturbed, often leading to conflict and regression. This effect can manifest in various ways:

1. **Weak Leadership:** A leader who succumbs to external pressures or internal biases may make decisions that undermine societal harmony. For instance, leaders who prioritize loyalty over competence often weaken institutions and erode public trust.
2. **Suppression of Truth:** Societies that suppress dissent or manipulate information create environments where falsehoods thrive. This can lead to widespread disillusionment and social fragmentation, as seen in propaganda-driven regimes.
3. **Overemphasis on Ideology:** When a single ideology dominates without room for alternative perspectives, it creates conditions for rebellion. For example, the rigid enforcement of Maoist policies during China's Cultural Revolution caused immense suffering and hindered progress.

Symptoms of Societal Upset

Unity vs. Unanimity: Understanding the Difference

There is a distinct difference between unity and unanimity in governance. Unity implies collective agreement on overarching goals, while unanimity demands complete conformity. The former is achievable and sustainable, while the latter is an unrealistic expectation that often leads to suppression of dissent.

Communist regimes, for example, have historically strived for unanimity by eliminating opposing voices. However, this has often resulted in long-term instability and eventual collapse, as seen in the disintegration of the Soviet Union. In contrast, democratic systems thrive on unity in diversity, where differing perspectives coexist within a framework of shared principles.

Solutions for Restoring Balance

To address the upsetting effect, societies must implement strategies that promote inclusion, dialogue, and justice:

1. **Encourage Transparency:** Open communication between leaders and citizens fosters trust and accountability.
2. **Support Diverse Voices:** Encouraging participation from all societal groups ensures that decisions reflect collective interests.
3. **Strengthen Institutions:** Robust legal and political frameworks provide stability and resilience against internal and external pressures.

By prioritizing these actions, societies can mitigate the upsetting effect and create conditions for sustained peace and prosperity. As the Bible teaches in **Isaiah 1:17**, *"Learn to do right; seek justice. Defend the oppressed. Take up the cause of the fatherless; plead the case of the widow."* This timeless wisdom underscores the importance of justice and compassion in governance.

When a society becomes destabilized, the symptoms manifest across various sectors and behaviors. Recognizing these indicators early can help leaders and institutions take corrective action:

1. **Faults in Governance and Systems:** Widespread inefficiencies in government operations and public services signal systemic issues. For instance, delays in disaster response or failure to maintain infrastructure often indicate deeper problems.
2. **Diminished Morale Among Citizens:** National crises can erode public confidence and courage, replacing resilience with fear and hesitation. For example, during economic recessions, citizens often feel disempowered, leading to inaction and despair.
3. **Blame-Shifting Among Individuals and Groups:** Instead of working collectively to solve problems, people may resort to blaming others, creating divisions and delaying solutions.
4. **Neglect of Duties:** A lack of accountability leads individuals to neglect their responsibilities while interfering in matters that do not concern them. This behavior exacerbates inefficiency and conflict.
5. **External Interference:** Weak nations often attract foreign exploitation or intervention. This is evident in countries with unstable governments, where external powers influence policies for their benefit.
6. **Declining Production:** Economic productivity suffers when societal divisions and unrest disrupt industries and labor. Historical examples include the collapse of major industries during prolonged conflicts like World War II.

7. **Polarization and Fragmentation:** Societal unity erodes as divisions deepen, often along political, ideological, or economic lines. This was seen in the fragmentation of Yugoslavia, where ethnic and nationalistic tensions led to the disintegration of the state.

Restoring Virtue and Stability

The analogy of a coin, with its two faces representing virtue and vice, is a useful framework for understanding societal balance. Virtue must be placed at the forefront of governance to ensure justice, equity, and progress. However, this requires deliberate effort to "screw" the coin securely in place, symbolizing strong institutional frameworks.

A Unitary Government's Role in Stability

A unitary form of government, though often more vulnerable to destabilization, can achieve stability through robust mechanisms. These include:

1. **Periodic Elections:** Democratic elections provide legitimacy and allow citizens to voice their concerns.
2. **Independent Institutions:** A strong judiciary, press, and legislative body act as checks on executive power.
3. **Autonomy:** Decentralizing authority ensures that diverse regional needs are met while maintaining national unity.

For example, the federal structure of Canada allows provinces significant autonomy while adhering to a cohesive national framework. This balance has contributed to Canada's stability and prosperity.

Adapting to a Rapidly Changing World

The modern world is evolving faster than ever, driven by technological advancements, globalization, and shifting demographics. To remain relevant and effective, governments must:

1. **Harness Natural Resources:** Effective resource management is critical for economic growth and sustainability.
2. **Provide Universal Education:** Access to quality education empowers citizens and reduces inequality.
3. **Ensure Swift Justice:** Transparent and efficient legal systems build public trust and deter corruption.
4. **Foster Inclusive Development:** Policies must promote equal opportunities across all segments of society.
5. **Uphold Dignity and Equality:** Recognizing and respecting cultural, linguistic, and ethnic diversity strengthens social cohesion.

Countries like Finland, known for their progressive policies in education and healthcare, exemplify how embracing these principles can lead to a high quality of life and international recognition.

Establishing Global Peace Through Local Virtue

Achieving peace on a global scale begins with fostering virtue and harmony within individual societies. When nations prioritize justice, equity, and collaboration, they set a precedent for international relations. As the Bible emphasizes in **James 3:18**, *"Peacemakers who sow in peace reap a harvest of righteousness."* By striving to embody these values, societies can contribute to a more just and peaceful world.

If we aim to establish such balance universally, peace at both local and global levels becomes not only possible but sustainable.

- **Disillusionment with Governance:** Apathy and distrust toward leadership are common when citizens feel unheard or oppressed.
- **Polarization:** Extreme divisions between groups indicate a lack of dialogue and understanding.
- **Suppression of Individual Freedom:** When individuals feel unable to express themselves or pursue their aspirations, societal progress stalls.
- **Widespread Cynicism:** A culture of negativity and hopelessness reflects deeper systemic issues.

Solutions for Restoring Balance

To address the upsetting effect, societies must implement strategies that promote inclusion, dialogue, and justice:

4. **Encourage Transparency:** Open communication between leaders and citizens fosters trust and accountability.
5. **Support Diverse Voices:** Encouraging participation from all societal groups ensures that decisions reflect collective interests.
6. **Strengthen Institutions:** Robust legal and political frameworks provide stability and resilience against internal and external pressures.

By prioritizing these actions, societies can mitigate the upsetting effect and create conditions for sustained peace and prosperity. As the Bible teaches in **Isaiah 1:17**, *"Learn to do right; seek justice. Defend the oppressed. Take up the cause of the fatherless; plead the case of the widow."* This timeless wisdom underscores the importance of justice and compassion in governance.

Managing Conflict Within Unions

Conflict is inevitable in any union, but it can be managed through mechanisms that promote dialogue and compromise. The key is to address grievances before they escalate into larger crises.

1. **Ventilation of Grievances:** Providing channels for individuals and groups to express their concerns helps prevent the buildup of tension. This principle is evident in the labor movement, where collective bargaining has historically been used to address workers' demands without resorting to strikes or violence.
2. **Encouraging Innovation:** Healthy competition within a union can drive innovation and progress. For example, the space race between the United States and the Soviet Union, though rooted in geopolitical rivalry, led to groundbreaking advancements in technology and science.
3. **Maintaining Flexibility:** A rigid union is more likely to break under pressure, while a flexible one can adapt to changing circumstances. The success of the Nordic model lies in its ability to balance social welfare with market-driven economic policies, demonstrating the importance of adaptability.

The Fabric of Society: Weaving Strength Through Diversity

The threads that bind a society—shared values, mutual respect, and a commitment to the common good—are what ensure its resilience. These threads must be continuously reinforced through education, dialogue, and cooperation.

The Bible offers wisdom in **Ecclesiastes 4:12**, *"Though one may be overpowered, two can defend themselves. A cord of three strands is not quickly broken."* This verse underscores the strength that comes from unity, reminding us that together, we can overcome even the greatest challenges.

The Importance of Balance and Opposition in Society

Societies thrive when there is a dynamic balance between opposing forces. The presence of both rightists and leftists, or contrasting ideologies, is not inherently detrimental; rather, it is a necessary condition for progress and growth. When balanced, these forces create momentum and foster dialogue, ensuring that no single viewpoint dominates unchecked.

For example, consider the interplay between innovation and tradition. Societies that value only tradition may stagnate, while those that dismiss tradition entirely risk losing their cultural identity. The United States, with its robust system of checks and balances, demonstrates how opposition and criticism can strengthen governance by preventing abuses of power and encouraging diverse perspectives.

Constructive Opposition: A Valve for Social Harmony

Opposition and criticism play a crucial role in maintaining societal equilibrium. They act as a safety valve, allowing grievances to be aired and addressed before they escalate into larger conflicts. As the Bible advises in **Proverbs 27:17**, *"As iron sharpens iron, so one person sharpens another."* Constructive criticism is essential for personal and societal growth.

In the past, societies that suppressed dissent often faced dire consequences. For instance, authoritarian regimes that silenced critics through violence or intimidation eventually collapsed under the weight of their unresolved tensions. In contrast, democracies that encourage open dialogue, such as Norway or Canada, have consistently ranked high in measures of social stability and happiness.

Reflection for Leaders

Effective leadership requires self-awareness and a commitment to balance. Leaders should regularly ask themselves:

1. **Am I prioritizing one side of a dichotomy at the expense of the other?**
2. **Have I created systems that are adaptable while maintaining stability?**
3. **How do I integrate diverse perspectives to ensure inclusivity and fairness?**

Conclusion: The Art of Equilibrium

Governance is the pursuit of equilibrium, an ongoing effort to balance competing forces in service of societal stability and progress. Like a tightrope walker navigating the fine line between stability and movement, leaders must balance tradition with innovation, individuality with unity, and freedom with responsibility.

Leadership in any society requires a delicate balance between decisiveness and openness to criticism. A wise leader listens to dissenting voices, using them to refine policies and address potential flaws. This approach not only strengthens governance but also builds trust and legitimacy.

History is replete with examples of leaders who thrived by embracing constructive criticism. Abraham Lincoln, during the American Civil War, famously surrounded himself with a "team of rivals"—individuals who challenged his views and helped him make better decisions. In contrast, leaders who insulated themselves from opposition, such as Louis XVI of France, often met with disastrous outcomes.

For leaders, the ability to separate personal ego from public service is paramount. By fostering an environment where criticism is welcomed and addressed, they can prevent the buildup of societal tensions and ensure long-term stability.

The greatest leaders understand that these forces are not enemies but interdependent allies. When managed wisely, dichotomies become sources of strength, driving societal growth and resilience. The lesson for leaders is simple yet profound: embrace the complexity of governance, for it is through balancing these tensions that true stability, harmony, and greatness are achieved.

Chapter 3: Positive Ideas – The Building Blocks of Progress

"An idea can transform a moment, define an era, and shape the destiny of nations."

Ideas are the unseen forces that guide humanity's trajectory, driving the progress of civilizations or plunging them into disarray. They transcend time and geography, leaving indelible marks on cultures, societies, and governance. Positive ideas—those grounded in truth, justice, equity, and inclusivity—are the cornerstones of thriving societies. They inspire innovation, foster unity, and pave pathways to resilience. Negative ideas, by contrast, breed division, erode trust, and stifle progress, undermining the very foundations of societal harmony.

This chapter examines the transformative power of positive ideas, the dangers posed by negative ones, and the role of leadership in cultivating and implementing ideas that propel humanity forward. Through historical examples, theoretical insights, and practical strategies, we explore how leaders can wield the power of ideas to drive progress.

The Nature of Positive Ideas

Positive ideas are the seeds of progress, serving as catalysts for transformation in both individual lives and broader societies. These ideas resonate across cultural, societal, and generational divides, inspiring collective action and nurturing an enduring sense of hope. They act as guiding principles, rooted in universal truths and actionable solutions, transcending momentary challenges to align humanity with enduring principles of fairness, growth, and shared prosperity.

By encouraging innovation and fostering collaboration, positive ideas become the bedrock of progress. They illuminate paths forward, even amidst uncertainty, and inspire people to work together toward common goals. Whether addressing immediate concerns or laying the foundation for long-term advancement, positive ideas have the power to unify and energize.

Characteristics of Positive Ideas

Truthfulness

Positive ideas are firmly anchored in facts, reality, and transparency. By fostering trust among individuals, institutions, and communities, they create an environment where informed decisions can thrive. Truth serves as the foundation of clarity, dispelling misinformation and building a shared understanding essential for collaboration. Positive ideas respect evidence and adapt to new insights, ensuring their relevance and credibility.

Justice and Equity

At their core, positive ideas prioritize fairness, ensuring opportunities, rights, and benefits are accessible to all. They aim to address systemic inequities by leveling the playing field for marginalized and underserved populations. By challenging unjust structures and advocating for inclusive policies, these ideas empower individuals and communities to reach their full potential while promoting a more equitable society.

Inclusivity

Positive ideas celebrate diversity in all its forms, recognizing that strength arises from embracing a spectrum of perspectives, experiences, and backgrounds. They actively work to break down barriers, bridging divides and fostering unity in diversity. Inclusivity ensures that no voice is overlooked, and every contribution is valued, enriching collective efforts with a broad array of insights and solutions.

Practicality

Positive ideas are not merely aspirational—they are actionable and grounded in practicality. They offer tangible solutions to pressing societal challenges, inspiring confidence in their feasibility and impact. Practicality ensures that these ideas are not only visionary but also implementable, allowing them to achieve meaningful outcomes in the real world. By addressing challenges with pragmatic strategies, positive ideas pave the way for sustainable progress.

Through these defining characteristics, positive ideas act as beacons of possibility, guiding humanity toward a future defined by fairness, unity, and shared growth. Their transformative power lies in their ability to connect, inspire, and mobilize individuals and communities, creating a collective momentum for a better tomorrow.

Historical Examples of Positive Ideas

History provides powerful examples of how positive ideas have reshaped societies, dismantled injustices, and spurred progress.

1. The Abolition of Slavery

Rooted in the belief in universal human rights, the abolitionist movement was one of history's most profound moral revolutions. Visionaries such as Frederick Douglass, William Wilberforce, and Harriet Tubman championed the idea that all humans are inherently equal, regardless of race or origin. This idea challenged centuries of institutionalized oppression, dismantling the legal and moral frameworks that had perpetuated slavery.

Impact:
The abolition of slavery not only transformed lives but also redefined societal values. It laid the
groundwork for ongoing struggles for racial justice, equality, and human dignity.

---

2. The Civil Rights Movement

The Civil Rights Movement of the mid-20th century in the United States serves as a profound
testament to the transformative power of positive ideas. Rooted in the fundamental principle of
justice for all, this movement sought to dismantle systemic racial inequities and create a society
where equality was not merely an aspiration but a lived reality. It challenged deeply entrenched
prejudices and discriminatory practices, uniting individuals across diverse backgrounds in
pursuit of fairness and human dignity.

At the forefront of this movement was Dr. Martin Luther King Jr., whose vision of a world
where individuals are judged by the content of their character rather than the color of their skin
became a beacon of hope and a call to action. His eloquence, courage, and unwavering
commitment to nonviolence galvanized millions, transcending racial, cultural, and national
boundaries. King's speeches, such as the iconic "I Have a Dream" address, articulated a
powerful and inclusive vision of justice that resonated deeply with people from all walks of life.

The movement was characterized by courageous acts of resistance and advocacy, from bus
boycotts and sit-ins to peaceful marches and legal challenges. Leaders and grassroots activists
alike displayed extraordinary resolve, often facing violence and oppression with unwavering
dignity. Their actions demonstrated the profound ability of positive ideas, rooted in truth and
justice, to challenge even the most formidable systems of injustice.

Impact of the Civil Rights Movement

The achievements of the Civil Rights Movement were monumental, reshaping the social,
political, and cultural fabric of the United States:

1. **Dismantling Segregationist Policies**
   The movement successfully overturned key elements of institutionalized racism, such as
   Jim Crow laws that enforced segregation. Landmark legislation, including the Civil
   Rights Act of 1964 and the Voting Rights Act of 1965, established legal protections
   against racial discrimination, laying the groundwork for greater equality and justice.
2. **Empowering Marginalized Communities**
   By challenging systemic barriers, the movement empowered African Americans and
   other marginalized groups to demand their rights and assert their place in society. This
   empowerment extended beyond legal victories, fostering a sense of pride, agency, and
   solidarity within these communities.
3. **Global Inspiration**
   The Civil Rights Movement inspired similar struggles for justice and equality around the
   world. From South Africa's anti-apartheid movement to various campaigns for

indigenous rights and gender equality, the principles and strategies employed by the Civil Rights Movement served as a blueprint for social change globally.

4. **Advancing Nonviolent Activism**
    The movement showcased the effectiveness of nonviolent resistance as a strategy for achieving systemic change. By adhering to principles of peaceful protest, it highlighted the moral strength of its cause and garnered widespread support from individuals and institutions worldwide.

5. **Cultural Transformation**
    The Civil Rights Movement profoundly influenced art, literature, and public discourse, encouraging a reevaluation of identity, justice, and the American ideal. It fostered a broader recognition of the contributions and experiences of African Americans, reshaping narratives in education, media, and cultural institutions.

The legacy of the Civil Rights Movement endures as a reminder of the enduring power of positive ideas to confront injustice and inspire transformation. It demonstrates that even in the face of seemingly insurmountable challenges, the pursuit of justice, equity, and human dignity can unite people, ignite change, and leave an indelible mark on history.

Key Insight for Leaders:

Positive ideas align with humanity's innate aspirations for dignity, fairness, and growth. Leaders who champion such ideas forge legacies of progress and unity.

The Threat of Negative Ideas

Negative ideas are insidious forces that exploit fear, prejudice, and misinformation, often presenting themselves as quick fixes or necessary solutions. Unlike the constructive nature of positive ideas, negative ideas are inherently corrosive, eroding societal stability, hindering progress, and perpetuating harm. They thrive in environments where trust is fragile and clarity is lacking, preying on human insecurities and vulnerabilities to gain acceptance and traction.

By masquerading as plausible solutions, negative ideas can infiltrate institutions, policies, and public discourse, often with devastating consequences. Their influence tends to amplify societal divisions, perpetuate inequities, and undermine long-term growth. The threat of negative ideas lies not only in their immediate impacts but also in their ability to leave lasting scars on the social fabric, creating challenges that span generations.

Characteristics of Negative Ideas

1. Deception

Negative ideas are built on distortion and manipulation. They twist facts, spread misinformation, and prey on ignorance to obscure reality and erode trust. By creating confusion and fostering doubt, these ideas make it difficult for individuals and communities to discern truth from falsehood, undermining informed decision-making. Deception fosters environments of suspicion, where fear and cynicism take root.

2. Division

Rather than fostering unity, negative ideas exploit differences—be they cultural, economic, religious, or ideological. By accentuating divisions, they sow discord, creating "us vs. them" mentalities that fracture communities. This divisiveness leads to polarization, making collaboration and mutual understanding nearly impossible, and often results in prolonged conflicts and animosities.

3. Injustice

Negative ideas prioritize the interests of a select few, often at the expense of the majority. They perpetuate systemic inequities by reinforcing power imbalances and enabling exploitation. Injustice becomes a recurring theme as these ideas deepen societal disparities, stifle upward mobility, and suppress marginalized voices.

4. Short-Term Focus

Negative ideas frequently present superficial fixes to complex problems, offering immediate gratification while ignoring or exacerbating long-term consequences. Their shortsightedness not only delays meaningful solutions but often leads to crises that require far greater effort and resources to address in the future.

Examples of Negative Ideas

1. Racial Supremacy

The ideology of racial superiority, most infamously exemplified by Nazi Germany, is a stark example of how negative ideas can devastate societies. The belief in racial hierarchy led to atrocities such as the Holocaust, where millions of lives were systematically exterminated, and to World War II, which caused untold suffering and global conflict. Beyond the immediate horrors, the ideology of racial supremacy left an enduring legacy of intergenerational trauma, social division, and a cautionary tale of the consequences of unchecked hate.

2. Economic Exploitation

Policies driven by greed, such as colonialism, exemplify the destructive power of negative ideas in economic systems. Colonialism exploited entire populations, drained natural resources, and imposed foreign dominance, leaving a legacy of poverty and inequality in many regions. The effects of these exploitative practices continue to ripple through modern economies, reinforcing systemic disparities and hindering sustainable development in formerly colonized nations.

3. Scapegoating

The practice of attributing societal problems to specific groups—whether immigrants, religious minorities, or other communities—has led to significant historical and contemporary harm. Scapegoating fuels prejudice, incites violence, and diverts attention from addressing root causes, weakening societal cohesion and perpetuating cycles of blame.

Key Insights for Leaders

Negative ideas often gain traction by exploiting vulnerabilities or presenting themselves as logical solutions in moments of uncertainty or crisis. Leaders must remain vigilant in identifying and countering these ideas to safeguard societal integrity. This vigilance involves fostering critical thinking, promoting transparency, and encouraging inclusive dialogue.

1. **Recognize Early Warning Signs**
   Negative ideas often begin subtly, gaining momentum under the guise of practicality or tradition. Leaders must actively challenge narratives that promote division, misinformation, or inequity.
2. **Promote Positive Alternatives**
   Countering negative ideas requires more than criticism; it involves presenting actionable, inclusive, and long-term solutions that address the underlying concerns negative ideas seek to exploit.
3. **Encourage Education and Awareness**
   An informed populace is less susceptible to deception. By prioritizing education and creating platforms for open discussion, leaders can foster resilience against divisive and harmful ideologies.

By remaining proactive and principled, leaders can prevent the spread of negative ideas, ensuring they do not derail societal progress or compromise the values of equity, unity, and sustainability.

The Interplay of Positive and Negative Ideas

Ideas rarely exist in isolation. Often, negative ideas piggyback on positive frameworks, distorting their potential and creating unintended consequences. Recognizing this interplay is crucial for leaders tasked with implementing transformative change.

Examples of the Interplay

1. **Paper Currency**
   Initially a positive innovation facilitating trade and economic growth, paper currency became problematic when mismanaged through inflationary policies and speculative markets.
2. **Globalization**
   While globalization has connected economies and lifted millions out of poverty, its negative aspects—such as exploitation of labor, environmental degradation, and cultural homogenization—stem from unbalanced implementation.

Key Insight for Leaders:

Leaders must evaluate both the short-term benefits and long-term consequences of ideas, ensuring they amplify progress rather than perpetuate harm.

Transforming Ideas into Movements

Ideas, no matter how powerful, require champions to transform them into movements. Leaders play a pivotal role in this process by articulating visions, mobilizing support, and institutionalizing change.

Case Study: The Women's Suffrage Movement

The fight for women's right to vote epitomizes how a positive idea can evolve into a transformative movement. Leaders like Susan B. Anthony, Emmeline Pankhurst, and Sojourner Truth articulated the idea of gender equality, mobilizing communities through advocacy, protests, and persistent efforts.

Impact:
The enfranchisement of women reshaped societal structures, empowering half the population to participate fully in democratic processes.

Steps to Transform Ideas into Movements

1. **Articulate a Clear Vision:**
   Define the idea's goals, values, and relevance. Use compelling narratives to connect emotionally with people.
2. **Mobilize Public Support:**
   Engage communities through campaigns, partnerships, and grassroots efforts. Highlight the idea's benefits and urgency.
3. **Institutionalize Change:**
   Embed the idea into policies, laws, and systems to ensure its longevity.

Key Insight for Leaders:

Movements thrive when they are rooted in clarity, inclusivity, and collective action. Leaders must build coalitions that amplify the idea's power and reach.

The Role of Leadership in Nurturing Ideas

Leadership is the catalyst that determines whether ideas flourish or falter. Visionary leaders align their strategies with positive ideals, inspiring trust, collaboration, and innovation. Conversely, authoritarian leaders suppress or distort ideas, stifling progress and perpetuating stagnation.

Case Study: Franklin D. Roosevelt's New Deal

During the Great Depression, Franklin D. Roosevelt turned the idea of economic recovery into actionable policies. The New Deal provided jobs, reformed financial systems, and restored hope to millions of Americans.

Key Lessons:

- Leaders must prioritize the collective good over personal ambition.
- By fostering dialogue and collaboration, leaders can transform challenges into opportunities.

Practical Framework for Leaders to Cultivate Positive Ideas

1. **Encourage Open Dialogue:**
   Create platforms for diverse voices to share insights, ensuring ideas are refined through constructive discourse.

2. **Champion Truth and Justice:**
   Align ideas with universal principles of fairness, transparency, and equity.
3. **Anticipate Resistance:**
   Expect opposition and develop strategies to address misinformation, fear, and skepticism.
4. **Build Institutional Support:**
   Establish policies and frameworks that institutionalize positive ideas, embedding them into the fabric of governance.

Reflections for Leaders

To evaluate the ideas driving your leadership, consider the following questions:

1. **Does this idea promote truth, justice, and inclusivity?**
2. **How does it address both immediate needs and long-term goals?**
3. **Have I engaged diverse perspectives to refine and strengthen the idea?**
4. **What mechanisms will ensure its sustainability?**

Conclusion: Ideas as Catalysts for Progress

Ideas are the lifeblood of governance and society. Positive ideas inspire hope, bridge divides, and shape civilizations that thrive. Leaders who champion such ideas build legacies rooted in equity, resilience, and progress. Conversely, negative ideas sow discord and stagnation, threatening the foundations of peace and prosperity.

The lesson is clear: leadership is not just about actions but about the ideas that drive them. Leaders must cultivate, champion, and implement ideas that uplift humanity, ensuring that progress is not only achieved but sustained. In the hands of visionary leaders, ideas become the building blocks of a better world.

Chapter 4: Accountability and Proportionality – Pillars of Governance

"Justice demands accountability, and progress thrives on proportionality."

Accountability and proportionality are the cornerstones of ethical and effective governance. These principles ensure that power is exercised responsibly, decisions are just, and resources are distributed fairly. Without accountability, governance risks devolving into unchecked corruption and authoritarianism. Without proportionality, policies become skewed, fostering inequity and discord. Together, these pillars uphold trust, equity, and the stability necessary for societal progress. Life often presents an array of challenges that demand resilience, wisdom, and a steadfast commitment to purpose. At times, individuals encounter opposition while striving to correct injustices or guide others toward righteousness. This process is fraught with difficulty, requiring immense courage, tact, and timely action.

It is common for close companions and loved ones to resist, sometimes unknowingly, the very changes that aim to improve their lives. However, this opposition should not discourage us. As seen throughout history, some individuals support and advocate for noble causes, acting as pillars of encouragement. Success often depends on unwavering determination to overcome the downward pull of adversity, counterbalanced by the upward pull of hope and faith.

This chapter delves into how accountability and proportionality shape governance, exploring historical examples, natural analogies, and modern practices. Leaders will find practical strategies to embed these principles in their approach, ensuring they build societies that are fair, resilient, and thriving.

The Role of Accountability in Governance

Accountability is the mechanism by which individuals and institutions are held responsible for their actions. It involves creating systems that monitor, evaluate, and correct the exercise of power, ensuring that it serves the collective good. Accountability fosters transparency, builds trust, and deters misconduct. Imagine the dynamic between two individuals engaged in a tug-of-war. The rope symbolizes life's constant tension, where one side pulls toward righteousness, and the other toward waywardness. This struggle is reflected in our daily interactions and decisions, where competing ideologies and values challenge our resolve.

The Dual Roles: The Checkers and the Checked

In every governance system, two critical roles exist:

1. **The Checkers**: Institutions and individuals tasked with oversight, such as the judiciary, media, civil society, and regulatory bodies.
2. **The Checked**: Those who wield power, including government officials, corporate leaders, and public servants.

These roles create a feedback loop that sharpens both parties. Proverbs 27:17 states, *"As iron sharpens iron, so one person sharpens another."* This dynamic ensures that power is tempered by scrutiny and accountability remains robust.

Historical Case Study: The Watergate Scandal

The Watergate scandal (1972–1974) exemplifies the critical role of accountability in governance. When journalists uncovered illegal activities tied to President Richard Nixon's administration, the subsequent investigations exposed corruption at the highest levels of power. Nixon ultimately resigned to avoid impeachment.

Key Insights:

- Independent institutions, such as the press and judiciary, are essential for exposing and addressing misconduct.
- Transparency and vigilance prevent abuses of power from festering unchecked.

Modern Example: Corporate Accountability

Corporate governance has increasingly emphasized accountability, particularly in addressing environmental and social responsibilities. Patagonia, an outdoor clothing company, exemplifies this approach by embedding sustainability and transparency into its operations. By openly reporting its environmental impact and engaging in ethical practices, Patagonia has built trust and loyalty among its stakeholders.

Key Insight for Leaders:
Accountability is not punitive but constructive. It fosters trust, collaboration, and innovation in both public and private sectors.

The Role of Proportionality in Governance

Proportionality ensures that actions, policies, and decisions are measured, fair, and just. It seeks a balance that avoids extremes and promotes equity, stability, and trust. Leaders who embrace proportionality create governance systems that reflect fairness and adaptability.

Proportionality in Nature

Nature offers powerful examples of proportionality, demonstrating how balance sustains ecosystems and life itself:

1. **The Balance of Ecosystems**: Predator-prey relationships maintain biodiversity and prevent overpopulation.
2. **The Composition of Air**: The precise mix of oxygen, nitrogen, and carbon dioxide sustains life without tipping into toxicity.

Governance, like nature, requires equilibrium. Policies and decisions must balance competing interests to ensure harmony and sustainability.

Proportionality in Law and Policy

1. Legal Proportionality

Injustice arises when punishments or legal measures disproportionately exceed the severity of crimes. A just system tailors responses to fit the circumstances.

Example:
Norway's rehabilitative prison system embodies legal proportionality. Instead of harsh punishments, the focus is on rehabilitation, education, and reintegration. This approach has resulted in one of the lowest recidivism rates globally, proving that proportional responses can foster societal stability.

2. Economic Proportionality

Economic policies must ensure that wealth distribution is equitable without stifling innovation or productivity.

Example:
The Nordic countries' progressive tax systems balance economic growth with robust social

welfare. These policies promote equity while maintaining high standards of living and global competitiveness.

Key Insight for Leaders:
Proportionality is essential for creating policies that reflect fairness, promote stability, and earn public trust.

The Consequences of Neglecting Accountability and Proportionality

When accountability and proportionality are disregarded, societies face significant risks. Below are three critical consequences:

---

1. Corruption and Mismanagement

Unchecked power leads to corruption, undermining public trust and eroding institutions.

Example:
Venezuela's economic collapse under Nicolás Maduro's leadership highlights the dangers of unchecked power. Rampant corruption, mismanagement of resources, and lack of accountability devastated the nation's economy and impoverished its population.

---

2. Social Inequity

Policies that lack proportionality exacerbate wealth gaps and fuel social unrest.

Example:
The French Revolution was catalyzed by disproportionate taxation and the concentration of wealth among the aristocracy. The stark inequality led to widespread discontent, culminating in a violent upheaval that reshaped French society.

---

3. Institutional Weakness

Systems that fail to hold leaders accountable become fragile, making them vulnerable to crises.

Example:
The 2008 collapse of Lehman Brothers, a major catalyst of the global financial crisis, revealed systemic failures in financial oversight. The lack of accountability in banking and investment practices triggered widespread economic turmoil.

Practical Frameworks for Accountability and Proportionality

The synthesis of proportionality and accountability often leads to growth and renewal. In the Christian tradition, this concept is epitomized by the cross, which unites the vertical connection between God and humanity with the horizontal bond between individuals. This powerful symbol reminds believers of their dual responsibilities: to love God and to love their neighbors.

When individuals and societies embrace this balance, they create an environment where virtues flourish, and conflicts are resolved. For instance, when leaders prioritize justice and compassion, they embody the proportionality of divine guidance while addressing the accountability needs of their communities.

Leaders can adopt specific strategies to uphold accountability and proportionality in governance:

1. Institutional Mechanisms

Establishing independent oversight bodies ensures that power is checked effectively.

Example:
Singapore's **Corrupt Practices Investigation Bureau (CPIB)** has been instrumental in maintaining one of the lowest corruption rates globally. Its independence and thorough investigation processes uphold transparency and accountability.

2. Transparent Governance

Embracing transparency fosters public trust by allowing citizens to monitor government actions.

Example:
Estonia's e-governance model is a leader in transparency. Citizens can access public records, monitor transactions, and even vote online, creating an environment of accountability and accessibility.

3. Inclusive Policymaking

Including diverse voices in decision-making ensures proportional representation and fair outcomes.

Example:
Rwanda's gender-balanced parliament has led to more inclusive and effective legislation. By prioritizing equity, the country has achieved notable progress in areas such as education and healthcare.

The Role of Technology in Strengthening Accountability

Technological advancements offer powerful tools to enhance accountability and proportionality. Leaders can harness these tools to improve governance efficiency and integrity.

1. Blockchain Technology

Blockchain ensures transparency by creating immutable records of transactions. This reduces opportunities for corruption in public and private sectors.

2. Artificial Intelligence (AI)

AI can monitor compliance with regulations, identify inefficiencies, and provide data-driven insights for fair policy implementation.

Key Insight for Leaders:
By leveraging technology, leaders can strengthen governance systems, making them more transparent, efficient, and equitable.

Reflection for Leaders

Leaders must continuously evaluate their adherence to accountability and proportionality. Reflecting on the following questions can guide decision-making:

1. **Are mechanisms in place to monitor and evaluate my decisions and actions?**
2. **Do my policies reflect fairness and inclusivity, or do they disproportionately benefit certain groups?**

3. **Am I transparent in my communication with stakeholders and the public?**
4. **How can I leverage technology to strengthen accountability and proportionality in governance?**

Conclusion: Building Trust Through Accountability and Proportionality

Accountability and proportionality are not abstract ideals; they are practical tools for fostering equity, stability, and progress. Leaders who embrace these principles demonstrate integrity and earn the confidence of their constituents. Conversely, governance without accountability becomes tyranny, and governance without proportionality fosters injustice.

Leadership, rooted in wisdom and righteousness, is vital to maintaining this balance. As Proverbs 11:14 advises, "Where there is no guidance, a people falls, but in an abundance of counselors there is safety." Leaders must seek truth, govern justly, and ensure that virtues outweigh vices.

When leaders fail, they leave room for chaos. This concept can be compared to the fall of the Roman Empire, where moral decay and internal divisions paved the way for its downfall. A society without moral and ethical checks soon collapses under the weight of its own vices.

By embedding accountability and proportionality into governance structures, leaders can build societies that are not only stable but also just and thriving. These principles ensure that power serves the people, decisions reflect fairness, and progress is both sustainable and inclusive. The lesson for leaders is clear: integrity and balance are the hallmarks of enduring governance.

Chapter 5: Ideologies and the Ripple Effect

"An ideology is like a pebble thrown into a pond—the ripples extend far beyond the initial impact."

At the heart of governance lies ideology—a complex and deeply influential set of beliefs, principles, and values that shape the decisions, policies, and societal structures of communities and nations. Ideologies act as the blueprints of governance, guiding leaders in shaping systems that determine how societies function. Positive ideologies can unify populations, inspire progress, and foster innovation. Negative ideologies, however, can polarize communities, incite oppression, and perpetuate conflict.

The challenge for leaders lies in navigating the immense ripple effects of ideologies. These effects extend far beyond their points of origin, shaping the fabric of societies, influencing neighboring regions, and affecting future generations. Leaders must grasp the dynamics of ideologies to harness their power effectively and manage their consequences responsibly. This chapter explores the nature of ideologies, their ripple effects, and the strategies leaders can employ to ensure these ideologies serve as forces of positive change.

The Nature of Ideologies

Ideologies provide the intellectual frameworks that allow societies to function cohesively. They define the principles of governance, guide policymaking, and inspire social and cultural norms. At their core, ideologies represent the collective aspirations and values of a group or society. However, ideologies are double-edged: while they can unite people around shared goals and foster progress, they can also divide and marginalize if applied dogmatically or rigidly.

Positive Ideologies

Positive ideologies serve as catalysts for societal advancement. Rooted in inclusivity, fairness, and collective well-being, they promote equity and cooperation while inspiring individuals and groups to achieve shared goals.

Characteristics of Positive Ideologies

1. **Inclusivity and Fairness**: They create systems where all individuals, regardless of background, can thrive and contribute meaningfully.
2. **Fostering Progress**: They prioritize the long-term advancement of society while addressing immediate challenges.
3. **Flexibility and Adaptability**: They evolve to meet the changing needs of societies, ensuring their relevance and sustainability.

Example: Democracy

Democracy exemplifies the transformative power of positive ideologies. It emphasizes representation, equality, and individual freedoms, allowing societies to reflect the will of their people. From the American and French revolutions to modern democratic movements worldwide, the democratic ideal has proven its capacity to unify diverse populations under shared values of justice and self-determination.

Negative Ideologies

Negative ideologies, by contrast, thrive on exclusion, division, and resistance to change. While they may offer temporary cohesion or stability for certain groups, their long-term consequences often perpetuate inequality, conflict, and oppression.

Characteristics of Negative Ideologies

1. **Exclusion and Marginalization**: They define "in-groups" and "out-groups," fostering societal divisions based on race, class, religion, or other factors.
2. **Division and Conflict**: They exploit fear and prejudice to consolidate power and achieve their goals.
3. **Resistance to Change**: They adhere rigidly to outdated principles, stifling progress and adaptability.

Example: Fascism

Fascism represents a historical example of a negative ideology. Its emphasis on authoritarian control, militaristic nationalism, and exclusionary policies led to catastrophic outcomes, including World War II and the Holocaust. The ripple effects of fascist regimes devastated entire populations and reshaped global geopolitics, leaving scars that are still evident today.

Key Insight for Leaders

Ideologies should be viewed as tools, not ends in themselves. Leaders must critically evaluate the outcomes of the ideologies they adopt, ensuring they prioritize adaptability, inclusivity, and the well-being of society over dogmatic adherence to doctrine.

The Ripple Effect of Ideologies

Ideologies rarely remain confined to their origins. Like a pebble dropped in water, their effects ripple outward, influencing societies, institutions, and global dynamics. These ripples can persist across decades or even centuries, shaping the course of history. For leaders, understanding the ripple effects of ideologies is essential to anticipating their consequences and managing their impacts responsibly. When a dominant ideology asserts itself, it naturally repels opposing ideas. This dynamic resembles the forces of magnetism, where like poles repel each other. As ideologies spread, they create tension at their borders, leading to zones of conflict. This tension is intensified by the population density, the geographic scope, and the acceptance or resistance of the ideology in question.

Over time, this force of repulsion weakens as ideological influence dissipates with distance and the passage of time. However, the regions near the borders of competing ideologies often bear the brunt of this clash. For instance, the Cold War created fault lines between the Soviet Union and Western-aligned nations, leading to hotspots like the Korean Peninsula, Vietnam, and Eastern Europe. These regions became battlegrounds not just for territorial control but for the assertion of ideological dominance.

The intensity of conflict is not uniform—it diminishes as the distance from the ideological epicenter increases. This phenomenon explains why border regions of historically opposing ideologies, such as North Korea and South Korea or Ukraine and Russia, remain hotspots of tension, while areas farther away experience less direct impact. In a way, these "borderlands" act as pressure points, absorbing and reflecting the ideological tensions of the larger powers they neighbor.

Historical Example: The Cold War

The Cold War provides a compelling example of the far-reaching ripple effects of ideological conflict. The ideological rivalry between capitalism and communism defined nearly every major international event from the late 1940s to the early 1990s.

Ripple Effects of Cold War Ideologies

1. **Proxy Wars**: Conflicts such as the Korean War, Vietnam War, and the Soviet-Afghan War were fueled by ideological competition between the United States and the Soviet Union.
2. **Economic Alliances**: Organizations like NATO and the Warsaw Pact aligned nations along ideological lines, creating spheres of influence that shaped global trade and diplomacy.
3. **Cultural Divisions**: The Iron Curtain became a powerful symbol of the ideological divide between Eastern and Western blocs, influencing cultural exchanges, education, and scientific collaboration.

Lessons for Leaders

- **Unchecked Ideological Rivalry Escalates Conflict**: Ideological competition often leads to division and violence when left unmanaged.

- **The Power of Diplomacy and Dialogue**: Leaders must prioritize diplomacy to mitigate the destructive effects of ideological clashes.
- **Recognizing Ideological Rigidity**: Leaders must identify when rigid adherence to ideology threatens stability and global cooperation.

Modern Example: Climate Change Ideologies

The global response to climate change offers a contemporary illustration of how ideological divides shape policy decisions and international relations. Differing ideologies about sustainability, economic growth, and environmental responsibility create ripples that influence industries, societies, and geopolitics.

Ripple Effects

1. **Global Agreements**: The Paris Agreement reflects the unifying power of pro-climate ideologies, bringing nations together to address a shared existential threat.
2. **Economic Transformation**: Renewable energy industries, driven by pro-environment ideologies, are reshaping global economies and job markets.
3. **Political Divides**: Ideological conflicts over climate policy influence elections, trade agreements, and international relations.

Key Insight for Leaders

Ideological ripples are inevitable, but their outcomes depend on how they are managed. Leaders must ensure that their ideologies foster collaboration, innovation, and resilience rather than division and stagnation.

The Spread and Adaptation of Ideologies

Ideologies are not static; they evolve as they spread, adapting to new contexts and inspiring fresh interpretations. This adaptability is both a strength and a challenge, as it allows ideologies to remain relevant while also creating opportunities for distortion or misuse.

The Role of Technology

Technology, particularly social media, has revolutionized the spread of ideologies. Platforms like Facebook, Twitter, and YouTube amplify ideological messages, enabling movements to gain global traction in unprecedented ways. However, these platforms also magnify misinformation, polarization, and ideological echo chambers.

Example: The Arab Spring

The Arab Spring demonstrated the power of technology to mobilize ideological movements. Social media enabled activists to organize protests, share information, and garner international attention. While the uprisings initially inspired hope, the lack of long-term planning in some regions underscored the challenges of sustaining ideological momentum.

Cultural Adaptation

Ideologies often blend with local traditions and values, creating unique hybrids that reflect the specific needs and identities of their contexts.

Example: Democracy in India

India's democratic model integrates Western governance principles with indigenous traditions such as the panchayat system of local self-government. This hybrid approach ensures that democracy resonates with India's diverse cultural and social landscape.

Key Insight for Leaders

Successful ideologies are adaptable. Leaders must ensure that their ideologies evolve to meet the needs of different societies while maintaining their core principles.

Managing Ideological Ripples

Leaders must actively manage the ripple effects of ideologies, balancing conviction with pragmatism. Thoughtful engagement with ideological differences is essential to prevent conflict and foster unity. When ideologies or policies are imposed forcibly on societies, the resulting upheaval affects not just the affected region but the entire interconnected world. As the Bible advises in **Romans 12:18**, *"If it is possible, as far as it depends on you, live at peace with everyone."*

By fostering dialogue, understanding, and cooperation, we can mitigate these ripples and work towards a more harmonious global community

1. Promote Open Dialogue

Encouraging debate and discussion allows leaders to address ideological differences constructively, fostering understanding and collaboration.

Example: South Africa's Truth and Reconciliation Commission

After the end of apartheid, South Africa's Truth and Reconciliation Commission provided a platform for victims and perpetrators to share their experiences. This process helped the nation heal by fostering transparency, accountability, and mutual understanding.

2. Build Inclusive Frameworks

Designing systems that accommodate diverse ideologies ensures that societies remain cohesive and collaborative.

Example: The European Union

The EU unites member states with differing political, economic, and cultural ideologies under shared goals such as economic prosperity and political stability. This inclusivity strengthens the bloc's resilience and influence on the global stage.

3. Emphasize Shared Values

Highlighting universal principles such as justice, equity, and sustainability can bridge ideological divides, fostering unity in diversity.

Example: The Universal Declaration of Human Rights

The Universal Declaration of Human Rights reflects shared human values, offering a foundation for international cooperation and consensus despite ideological differences.

Reflections for Leaders

Leaders must continuously evaluate the ideologies shaping their governance. Reflecting on the following questions can help ensure their ideologies remain forces of positive change:

1. **Does this ideology include or exclude certain groups? Why?**
2. **What ripple effects might this ideology have beyond its immediate application?**
3. **How can this ideology adapt to align with evolving societal needs?**
4. **Am I prepared to manage the challenges of ideological competition?**

Conclusion: Ideologies as Forces of Change

Ideologies are neither inherently good nor bad—they are tools shaped by their application. Leaders who understand the ripple effects of their ideologies can harness their power to inspire progress, mitigate conflict, and foster unity.

The lesson is clear: governance is not just about adopting an ideology but about managing its influence responsibly. By prioritizing adaptability, inclusivity, and collaboration, leaders can ensure their ideologies serve as catalysts for positive change. In doing so, they create ripples that extend far beyond their immediate context, shaping a better world for future generations.

Chapter 6: Building Alliances – Cooperation Without Exploitation

"True alliances are built on mutual respect, shared goals, and equitable benefits."

Alliances have played a pivotal role in shaping history, from ancient coalitions to modern international institutions. They are the threads that weave nations, organizations, and communities together, enabling them to achieve goals that no single entity could accomplish alone. However, the effectiveness and longevity of an alliance depend on its foundation. Alliances rooted in mutual respect, shared objectives, and equitable benefits foster trust, innovation, and progress. Conversely, alliances driven by exploitation or imbalance breed resentment, fragility, and eventual collapse.

The utility of alliance lies in its affirmation. When a speaker communicates with conviction, their words inspire and resonate among listeners. However, the permanence of this impact relies on how the alliance is sustained and propagated. Consider a leader such as Abraham Lincoln, whose affirmation of equality and unity during a tumultuous time defined the moral compass of a nation. His speeches, such as the Gettysburg Address, continue to affirm the truth of liberty and justice.

Alliance does not operate in isolation; it requires a constant sifting of falsehoods to maintain its purity. A leader who speaks the truth will often face opposition, but this tension sharpens and strengthens the affirmation of alliance, creating a robust foundation for growth. Just as the Apostle Paul emphasized the necessity of testing all things and holding fast to what is good (1 Thessalonians 5:21), societies must consistently evaluate their values against a moral and truthful standard.

When the pursuit of truth falters, society risks succumbing to falsehoods that weaken its core. If a speaker does not continue to affirm and refine their alliance, their message may stagnate, leading to disillusionment. For instance, Martin Luther King Jr.'s persistence in reiterating the ideals of nonviolence and equality kept his message alive, even amid resistance. His truth was not static; it evolved through interaction with opposition and refinement of purpose.

Building equitable alliances requires thoughtful leadership, guided by principles of fairness, transparency, and cultural sensitivity. This chapter explores the nature of alliances, historical and modern lessons, and actionable frameworks to create partnerships that promote cooperation without exploitation.

Maintaining a Unified Society:

To ensure the continued success of an alliance:

- Criticism from within should be encouraged to foster improvement and growth.
- Leaders must safeguard the interests of all members and avoid polarization.
- Goals must evolve to address new challenges as initial objectives are met.

For example, leaders like Franklin D. Roosevelt adapted national goals during the Great Depression, maintaining societal alliance by addressing pressing economic challenges. Similarly, modern leaders must recognize the importance of evolving priorities while keeping foundational values intact.

Challenges and Opposites:

Progress is always accompanied by opposing forces. For every effort toward alliance, there may be counterforces seeking to divide. This dynamic is natural and should not be feared but rather managed with wisdom. For instance, the Civil Rights Movement faced resistance, yet it persevered through moral clarity and strategic action, ultimately reshaping societal values.

By fostering alliance rooted in shared interests, values, and adaptability, societies can navigate the complexities of human relationships, ensuring both progress and stability.

Maintaining alliance and Balance

1. **Importance of Polarization and Criticism:**
   - If polarization is managed effectively and criticism is encouraged constructively, an institution benefits from prosperity, progress, and stability. A balance between opposing forces is key to maintaining harmony.
2. **Formation of Artificial alliance:**
   - Artificial unions must emulate natural ones to ensure stability and progress.
   - Individuals excluded from alliance should form groups of critics to channel constructive opposition. Otherwise, crises and instability will ensue.
3. **Consequences of Ignoring Criticism:**
   - Disruption in the entire organization.
   - Erosion of trust among members.
   - Unforeseen disasters (e.g., natural or social calamities).
   - Institutional instability and insecurity.

Cultural and Historical Pride in alliance

1. **Role of Language and Culture:**
   - Shared language and culture serve as unifying forces. They foster mutual understanding and solidarity.
   - Common historical pride strengthens group identity and helps repel opposing forces.
2. **Tendency Toward Division:**
   - Cultural differences or conflicting historical narratives may lead to repulsion and fragmentation within groups.
   - Such tendencies necessitate efforts to bridge divides and create inclusive unions.

Interdependence of Sources of Interest

1. **Nature of Cooperation**
   People cooperate best when their interests are interconnected. Cooperation thrives when one individual's need leads them to collaborate with another who has complementary needs. Mutual respect and assistance grow from this connection. A society that disregards these interconnections risks losing its foundational strength. Self-sufficiency in isolation leads to disintegration; rather, each person must rely on others to sustain shared goals and visions.
2. **Role of Interdependence**
   Interdependence fosters unity within families, communities, and nations. By building trust and mutual reliance, individuals and groups function as harmonious entities. This process ensures a balance between needs and resources, promoting shared growth. When interdependence falters, the social structure weakens, creating conflicts and inefficiencies.
3. **Institutional Responsibility**
   Governments and institutions must embody principles of interdependence in their frameworks. Harmonized regulations and cooperative systems ensure the efficient functioning of society's various sectors—be it businesses, education, or civic organizations. Following natural laws of coexistence creates synergy and collective advancement.
4. **Consequences of Neglect**
   Without interdependence, communities fracture into competing groups, each pulling in separate directions. Such discord leads to social, economic, and moral degradation, weakening the entire societal fabric.
5. **Lessons from Nature**
   Nature exemplifies the power of balance and cooperation. Just as ecosystems thrive through intricate interdependencies, human organizations must model their systems to mirror these principles, fostering enduring connections that sustain all aspects of life.

The Nature of Alliances

At their core, alliances are agreements between two or more entities—nations, corporations, or communities—formed to achieve shared objectives. They often arise from a recognition of mutual interdependence, where collaboration is necessary to address challenges or seize opportunities. The most successful alliances rest on three key pillars:

1. **Mutual Benefit**: Each party gains value from the alliance, ensuring that collaboration remains worthwhile.
2. **Equity**: Power, resources, and responsibilities are distributed fairly, preventing domination by any one party.
3. **Trust**: Relationships are underpinned by transparency, accountability, and a commitment to shared goals.

Historical Perspectives on Alliances

History offers numerous examples of alliances that demonstrate the principles of success—and the consequences of failure.

The Success of NATO

The North Atlantic Treaty Organization (NATO), established in 1949, is a prime example of a successful alliance. Born out of the aftermath of World War II, NATO united its members around shared principles of collective defense, political stability, and resource-sharing. Its strength lies in its equitable distribution of responsibilities and a clear purpose: ensuring the security of its members.

Key Lessons:

- **Collective Goals Drive Longevity**: NATO's success is rooted in its shared objective of mutual defense, fostering unity among diverse nations.
- **Shared Resources Strengthen Alliances**: Member states contribute equitably, ensuring that no single country bears an undue burden.

The Downfall of the Warsaw Pact

In contrast, the Warsaw Pact, formed in 1955 as a counterbalance to NATO, exemplifies an alliance built on coercion rather than cooperation. Dominated by the Soviet Union, the pact's unequal power dynamics and forced participation fostered resentment among its member states. Its collapse in 1991 highlighted the fragility of alliances that prioritize domination over mutual respect.

Key Lessons:

- **Coercion Undermines Alliances**: Partnerships built on force rather than voluntary cooperation are inherently unstable.
- **Imbalanced Power Dynamics Create Fragility**: Exploitative relationships lead to mistrust and eventual fragmentation.

Key Insight for Leaders

Alliances thrive when they are built on shared values and voluntary participation. Leaders must prioritize collaboration over domination and seek equitable arrangements that benefit all parties involved.

Principles for Building Equitable Alliances

To build alliances that endure and promote progress, leaders must adhere to core principles that foster fairness, transparency, and mutual benefit.

1. Establish Clear Objectives

Defining the purpose and goals of an alliance ensures alignment among all parties from the outset. Ambiguity in objectives often leads to misunderstandings and conflicts.

Example: The European Union

The European Union (EU) was founded on principles of economic integration and peace. By establishing clear objectives—such as fostering free trade, promoting human rights, and ensuring political stability—the EU aligned the interests of its member states, enabling them to work collectively toward shared goals.

Actionable Steps:

- Convene initial discussions to define the alliance's mission and priorities.
- Draft a formal agreement that outlines objectives, responsibilities, and expected outcomes.

2. Balance Power Dynamics

Ensuring that no single entity dominates the alliance fosters trust and equitable decision-making. When power imbalances persist, alliances risk becoming exploitative or unstable.

Example: ASEAN

The Association of Southeast Asian Nations (ASEAN) operates on a principle of consensus, ensuring that all member states, regardless of size or economic power, have an equal voice in decision-making. This approach has helped ASEAN maintain cohesion while addressing regional challenges collaboratively.

Actionable Steps:

- Create governance structures that promote equal representation in decision-making processes.
- Regularly review and adjust power dynamics to reflect the evolving needs of all members.

3. Prioritize Transparency

Transparency is the bedrock of trust. Open communication and accountability prevent misunderstandings and ensure that all parties remain aligned.

Example: The Paris Agreement

The Paris Agreement's transparency framework encourages countries to disclose their climate actions and progress toward agreed goals. This openness fosters accountability and builds trust among participating nations.

Actionable Steps:

- Implement mechanisms for regular reporting and information sharing.
- Use digital tools to provide real-time updates on alliance activities and outcomes.

Case Study: The Marshall Plan

The Marshall Plan, implemented after World War II, exemplifies an alliance rooted in generosity, mutual benefit, and shared goals. By providing economic aid to European nations, the United States helped rebuild war-torn economies, stabilize political systems, and foster long-term partnerships.

Key Outcomes

1. **Economic Growth**: Revitalized industries and infrastructure, laying the foundation for post-war prosperity.
2. **Strengthened Relationships**: Built trust between the U.S. and European nations, fostering long-term alliances.
3. **Avoidance of Exploitation**: Aid was provided with minimal conditions, prioritizing mutual recovery over dominance.

Key Insight

Alliances built on generosity and shared goals yield long-term benefits, both economically and diplomatically. Leaders must focus on fostering relationships that prioritize collective progress over immediate gain.

The Dangers of Exploitation in Alliances

When alliances are rooted in exploitation, they foster resentment, undermine trust, and ultimately collapse. Exploitation often arises when one party prioritizes its interests over the collective good, creating imbalances that destabilize partnerships.

Historical Example: Colonial Alliances

Colonial empires often established exploitative alliances with indigenous populations, extracting resources and labor while providing little in return. These imbalanced relationships prioritized the interests of colonial powers, leading to widespread resistance, economic disparity, and eventual decolonization.

Modern Example: Unequal Trade Agreements

Some modern trade agreements disproportionately benefit wealthier nations, leaving developing countries at a disadvantage. Such arrangements perpetuate global inequality and hinder sustainable development.

Key Insight for Leaders

Exploitative alliances may yield short-term gains but undermine long-term stability and trust. Leaders must prioritize equity and fairness to ensure the longevity of their partnerships.

People collaborate effectively only when their interests are mutually dependent. For instance, if person A meets their needs through person B, and person B reciprocates by fulfilling their needs with person A, a mutual respect and cooperation ensue. This forms the bedrock of social harmony. Dependence fosters alliance, creating systems that enable collective growth and shared success.

Conversely, if individuals are entirely self-sufficient and reject interdependence, society risks disintegration. This fragmentation halts cooperation, resulting in inefficiency. Nature teaches us to embrace interdependence, seen in all biological systems and organizational structures. Without this glue, entities pursue disparate directions, causing conflict and degradation. Alliance, when managed well, fosters productivity, harmony, and societal stability.

Confidence In Leadership

In challenging times, people naturally look toward their leaders for guidance, advice, and direction. A competent leader is one who commands the trust and confidence of their followers. The leader must embody a vision that resonates with the aspirations of their people. Their words and deeds should be consistent, conveying an unwavering determination to uphold the collective interests of their community or nation.

A leader who maintains the distinct identity of their people, while respecting others, fosters national pride and independence. If they compromise their principles, allowing others to dictate their course, it leads to a gradual decline of their leadership's credibility. A nation led by a weak leader is akin to a boat drifting without direction, leaving it vulnerable to external pressures.

In an effective leadership framework:

- **Trust is central**: A leader must earn the trust of their people by acting with integrity and foresight.
- **Criticism is embraced**: Criticism, even from opposition, is seen as a tool to refine policies and actions.
- **Strength lies in alliance**: Leaders who unite people under a shared vision can overcome differences and achieve greater goals.

Frameworks for Sustainable Alliances

Leaders can adopt the following frameworks to build alliances that are equitable, effective, and enduring:

---

1. Foster Inclusive Decision-Making

Inclusive decision-making ensures that all voices are heard and respected, preventing marginalization and fostering a sense of ownership among all parties.

Example: The African Union

The African Union's principle of rotating leadership ensures that all member states, regardless of size or influence, have equal opportunities to shape the organization's direction.

Actionable Steps:

- Establish councils or committees that include representatives from all parties.
- Rotate leadership roles to ensure equitable participation.

---

2. Share Risks and Rewards

Alliances thrive when risks and rewards are distributed equitably. Sharing benefits and responsibilities strengthens trust and ensures that all parties remain committed.

Example: Renewable Energy Partnerships

In many renewable energy projects, such as solar farm initiatives, profits are often shared with local communities. This approach fosters goodwill, promotes sustainability, and ensures that all stakeholders benefit from the alliance.

Actionable Steps:

- Develop profit-sharing models that reflect each party's contributions.
- Allocate resources and responsibilities proportionately to ensure balance.

---

3. Build Mechanisms for Conflict Resolution

Conflicts are inevitable in any alliance. Establishing fair and transparent systems for resolving disputes prevents fractures and strengthens the partnership.

Example: The World Trade Organization (WTO)

The WTO provides a structured dispute resolution mechanism for member nations, ensuring that conflicts are addressed through dialogue and negotiation rather than unilateral action.

Actionable Steps:

- Create a formal dispute resolution process with clear guidelines and timelines.
- Appoint neutral mediators or arbiters to oversee conflict resolution.

The Role of Cultural Sensitivity in Alliances

Cultural sensitivity is essential for building alliances that respect and celebrate diversity. Ignoring cultural differences can lead to misunderstandings, tensions, and breakdowns in communication.

Case Study: United Nations Peacekeeping Missions

United Nations peacekeeping missions often involve personnel from diverse cultural backgrounds. Successful missions prioritize cultural sensitivity training, ensuring effective collaboration and communication among teams.

Actionable Steps:

- Provide cultural awareness training for all alliance members.
- Incorporate diverse perspectives into decision-making processes.

Key Insight

Cultural sensitivity fosters trust, understanding, and cooperation, strengthening the foundation of alliances and enabling them to thrive in diverse contexts.

Technology and Modern Alliances

Technology has transformed the way alliances are formed, managed, and maintained. Leaders must leverage digital tools to enhance collaboration, transparency, and security.

Applications of Technology in Alliances

1. **Digital Platforms**: Facilitate real-time communication, decision-making, and resource allocation.
2. **Data Sharing**: Enable transparent tracking of progress and resource distribution.
3. **Cybersecurity Partnerships**: Protect shared digital infrastructures from external threats.

Example: The Five Eyes Alliance (FVEY)

The Five Eyes Alliance, an intelligence-sharing network among five countries, demonstrates how technology enhances global security cooperation by enabling seamless communication and data sharing.

Reflection for Leaders

To evaluate the strength and fairness of your alliances, consider the following questions:

1. **Are all parties benefiting equitably from this alliance?**
2. **Are power dynamics balanced, or does one entity dominate the relationship?**
3. **Have we established systems to address conflicts and ensure transparency?**
4. **How are cultural differences being acknowledged and respected?**

Conclusion: The Power of Fair Alliances

Alliances are among the most powerful tools for achieving collective progress. When built on mutual respect, shared goals, and equitable benefits, they become catalysts for innovation, peace, and stability. However, alliances rooted in exploitation or imbalance are destined to fail, leaving distrust and disarray in their wake.

The lesson is clear: alliances are partnerships, not hierarchies. Leaders who prioritize fairness, transparency, and collaboration will create alliances that stand the test of time, driving progress and prosperity for all involved. True alliances, grounded in equity and respect, are the foundation of sustainable development and global harmony.

Chapter 7: Sustainability and Resource Management

"The true test of leadership is not just how we use resources today but how we ensure their abundance for tomorrow."

Sustainability and resource management lie at the heart of effective governance. The ability to manage natural, economic, and human resources responsibly determines the quality of life for current and future generations. Leaders must address the pressing challenges of balancing economic growth with environmental stewardship and social equity, crafting policies that ensure resources are used wisely and replenished wherever possible.

This chapter delves into the principles of sustainability, lessons from history, and actionable strategies for resource management. By adopting sustainable practices and prioritizing equitable resource distribution, leaders can create societies that are resilient, prosperous, and harmonious.

The Importance of Sustainability

Sustainability refers to the capacity to meet present needs without compromising the ability of future generations to meet their own. It encompasses three interconnected pillars:

1. **Environmental Stewardship**: Protecting ecosystems, biodiversity, and natural resources.
2. **Economic Responsibility**: Promoting long-term growth over short-term exploitation.
3. **Social Equity**: Ensuring fair access to resources and opportunities for all members of society.

Why Sustainability Matters

1. **Finite Resources**
   Many natural resources, such as fossil fuels and freshwater, are nonrenewable or limited. Overexploitation depletes these resources, threatening the stability of ecosystems and economies alike.
2. **Global Interdependence**
   In an interconnected world, resource scarcity in one region often creates ripple effects that impact global trade, security, and social stability.
3. **Moral Responsibility**
   Future generations depend on today's leaders to make decisions that safeguard the planet and its resources. Sustainability is not just an economic necessity but an ethical imperative.

Key Insight for Leaders

Sustainability is not optional; it is an ethical and practical necessity. Leaders must adopt a forward-thinking mindset, crafting policies that balance immediate needs with long-term resilience.

Lessons from Nature: The Flow of Resources

Nature offers a powerful blueprint for sustainable resource management. Its cycles and systems demonstrate the principles of balance, replenishment, and interdependence:

1. **The Water Cycle**
   Water circulates through evaporation, condensation, and precipitation, ensuring continuous availability. This cycle teaches leaders the importance of creating systems that replenish resources while meeting human needs.
2. **Ecosystem Balance**
   In natural ecosystems, predator-prey relationships maintain population equilibrium, preventing overconsumption and resource depletion.

Application to Governance

Leaders can draw inspiration from these natural cycles to design policies and systems that align resource use with replenishment. For example:

- **Water Management**: Implementing rainwater harvesting and recycling systems to ensure sustainable freshwater supplies.
- **Agricultural Practices**: Encouraging crop rotation and soil conservation to maintain long-term productivity.

Historical Examples of Resource Management

1. The Dust Bowl (1930s)

During the Great Depression, unsustainable farming practices and over-farming in the United States led to severe soil erosion, creating one of the worst environmental disasters in history. Crops failed, families were displaced, and the economy suffered.

Lesson:
Sustainable agricultural practices, such as crop diversification and soil conservation, are essential to prevent long-term harm to ecosystems and communities.

---

2. Singapore's Water Strategy

Singapore, with limited natural freshwater resources, faced significant challenges in water management. Through innovative policies, it developed a comprehensive system that includes rainwater harvesting, desalination, and water recycling.

Outcome:
Singapore is now a global leader in water sustainability, ensuring resilience against resource scarcity.

Lesson:
Proactive and innovative strategies can turn resource constraints into opportunities for leadership and growth.

Key Insight

Resource mismanagement leads to disaster, while forward-thinking and innovative strategies ensure resilience and prosperity.

Modern Challenges in Resource Management

Leaders today face a range of complex challenges in managing resources sustainably. These include:

---

1. Climate Change

Rising global temperatures, sea-level rise, and extreme weather events threaten natural and human systems. Resource management must prioritize conservation, adaptation, and renewable energy solutions.

Example:
The Netherlands' flood management system combines engineering with natural solutions, such as wetlands restoration, to mitigate flooding and protect coastal areas.

2. Overpopulation and Urbanization

Rapid population growth and urbanization strain resources like water, food, and energy, particularly in developing regions.

Example:
India's Smart Cities Mission uses technology to optimize resource use in urban areas, improving efficiency and sustainability.

3. Inequality in Resource Distribution

Wealth disparities often lead to unequal access to essential resources, exacerbating social tensions and instability.

Example:
Land redistribution policies in Zimbabwe, while well-intentioned, failed due to poor planning and implementation, highlighting the importance of equitable yet carefully managed reforms.

Key Insight

Sustainable resource management must address not only environmental concerns but also the social and economic inequalities that arise from resource scarcity.

Principles for Sustainable Resource Management

To create resilient systems, leaders must embrace the following principles:

1. Reduce, Reuse, Recycle

Adopt circular economic models where resources are reused and waste is minimized.

Example:
Sweden's waste-to-energy program recycles nearly all municipal waste, converting it into energy to power homes and industries.

2. Invest in Renewable Resources

Transitioning from nonrenewable to renewable energy sources is critical for long-term sustainability.

Example:
Costa Rica generates over 99% of its electricity from renewable sources, positioning itself as a global leader in sustainable energy.

3. Empower Local Communities

Engaging local communities in resource management ensures solutions are culturally relevant and effective.

Example:
Kenya's community-led wildlife conservation programs protect biodiversity while supporting local livelihoods through ecotourism and sustainable practices.

Key Insight

Sustainability requires systemic change at every level—from national policies to grassroots initiatives.

Case Study: The Green Revolution

The Green Revolution of the mid-20th century transformed global agriculture through technological advancements such as high-yield crops, modern irrigation techniques, and chemical fertilizers. While it alleviated hunger for millions, it also created significant challenges:

1. **Depletion of Soil Nutrients**: Over-reliance on chemical inputs damaged soil health.
2. **Water Scarcity**: Intensive irrigation strained freshwater resources.
3. **Environmental Harm**: Increased use of pesticides and fertilizers led to pollution and biodiversity loss.

Lessons for Leaders

Technological advancements must be paired with sustainable practices to avoid long-term harm. Policies should balance immediate gains with the preservation of natural resources.

The Role of Technology in Sustainability

Technological innovation is a powerful tool for addressing resource challenges. By leveraging advancements in science and engineering, leaders can develop more efficient and sustainable systems.

---

1. Smart Agriculture

Precision farming techniques use data and technology to optimize resource use and reduce waste.

Example:
Drones and sensors in farming enhance crop yields while conserving water and fertilizers, minimizing environmental impact.

---

2. Energy Storage

Advances in battery technology enable the wider adoption of renewable energy by stabilizing power grids and storing excess energy.

Example:
Tesla's battery systems support renewable energy integration, promoting sustainable energy solutions.

---

3. Artificial Intelligence

AI models analyze resource needs, predict shortages, and optimize distribution.

Example:
AI-powered water management systems in California reduce waste and improve efficiency by analyzing consumption patterns.

Key Insight

Technology is a catalyst for sustainability, but its implementation must be guided by ethical and equitable principles.

Building Global Alliances for Sustainability

Resource management is a global challenge that requires international collaboration. No single nation can address issues like climate change, water scarcity, or biodiversity loss alone.

1. The Paris Agreement

The Paris Agreement unites nations in addressing climate change through shared goals and commitments to reduce carbon emissions.

2. The United Nations' Sustainable Development Goals (SDGs)

The SDGs provide a comprehensive framework for achieving global sustainability by 2030, addressing issues ranging from clean energy to responsible consumption.

Key Insight

Global challenges demand global solutions. Leaders must foster international cooperation to address resource management issues effectively.

Practical Frameworks for Leaders

To implement sustainable resource management, leaders can adopt the following strategies:

1. Establish Regulatory Frameworks

Enforce policies that limit overextraction, protect ecosystems, and encourage sustainable practices.

Example:
Norway's sovereign wealth fund invests oil revenues in sustainable projects, ensuring long-term economic and environmental benefits.

---

2. Encourage Public Participation

Educate citizens about sustainability and involve them in decision-making processes.

Example:
Japan's community-led disaster preparedness programs integrate local knowledge and participation, fostering resilience and engagement.

---

3. Incentivize Innovation

Provide financial incentives for businesses and individuals to adopt sustainable technologies.

Example:
Germany's subsidies for renewable energy have transformed the nation into a leader in sustainability, reducing its reliance on fossil fuels.

Reflection for Leaders

To assess your approach to sustainability and resource management, consider the following questions:

1. **Are my policies addressing short-term needs without compromising long-term sustainability?**
2. **Have I engaged stakeholders, including local communities, in resource management?**
3. **Am I investing in technologies and practices that replenish resources rather than deplete them?**

Conclusion: A Legacy of Sustainability

Resource management is about more than survival; it is about creating a legacy of abundance, equity, and resilience. Leaders who prioritize sustainability ensure not only the well-being of their constituents but also the health of the planet for generations to come.

The lesson is clear: resources are finite, but human ingenuity is boundless. By embracing sustainable practices, fostering innovation, and building global alliances, leaders can turn challenges into opportunities. In doing so, they pave the way for a future where both people and the planet thrive.

Chapter 8: Ethical Leadership in a Polarized World

"Ethics is the compass that guides leaders through the storms of division."

The modern world is fraught with divisions—political, economic, cultural, and ideological. Polarization has grown into a pervasive force, threatening to fragment societies, undermine trust, and stall collective progress. Leaders face the daunting task of navigating these divisions while fostering unity, promoting justice, and upholding ethical standards.

Ethical leadership is more critical than ever. It is the practice of governing with integrity, fairness, and accountability, prioritizing the collective good over individual or partisan interests. Ethical leaders must have the courage to stand firm in their values while being flexible enough to engage diverse perspectives. In this chapter, we explore the principles of ethical leadership, the challenges posed by polarization, and actionable strategies for building bridges in a divided world.

The Foundations of Ethical Leadership

Ethical leadership is rooted in a commitment to doing what is right, even when it is difficult or unpopular. It prioritizes the needs of the many over the desires of the few and seeks to create environments where collaboration and trust can flourish. Ethical leaders understand that their decisions carry far-reaching consequences and approach their roles with humility and responsibility.

Core Principles of Ethical Leadership

1. **Integrity**
   Acting consistently with moral and ethical standards, even in the face of opposition or adversity. Integrity builds trust and sets the foundation for credibility.

   Example:
   Angela Merkel, during her tenure as German Chancellor, demonstrated unwavering commitment to humanitarian values during the European refugee crisis. Despite political backlash, she prioritized compassion and human rights, welcoming over a million refugees into Germany.

2. **Transparency**
   Sharing information openly and honestly to build trust and reduce misunderstandings. Transparency ensures accountability and fosters a sense of inclusion among stakeholders.

   Example:
   New Zealand's response to COVID-19 emphasized clear, transparent communication. Prime Minister Jacinda Ardern provided regular updates with honesty and empathy, earning public confidence and compliance with pandemic measures.

3. **Empathy**
   Understanding and addressing the needs, fears, and aspirations of diverse groups. Empathy enables leaders to bridge divides and create solutions that resonate with all stakeholders.

   Example:
   Nelson Mandela's emphasis on reconciliation during South Africa's transition from apartheid showed deep empathy for both victims and perpetrators, paving the way for national healing.

Key Insight for Leaders

Ethics is not optional—it is the foundation of effective and lasting leadership. Leaders who embody integrity, transparency, and empathy inspire trust and drive progress even in the most challenging circumstances.

The Challenges of Polarization

Polarization divides societies into opposing camps, often creating an "us vs. them" mentality. It reduces the willingness to collaborate or compromise and fosters environments where misinformation, distrust, and hostility thrive.

Sources of Polarization

1. **Economic Inequality**
   Disparities in wealth and opportunity create resentment, fostering divisions between the privileged and the marginalized.

Example:
The Occupy Wall Street movement underscored the growing divide between the "1%" and the rest of society, fueling widespread frustration with systemic inequality.

---

2. Cultural Differences

Conflicts over identity, religion, or values deepen societal fractures.

Example:
Immigration debates in the U.S. and Europe have polarized populations, with one side emphasizing security and cultural preservation, while the other advocates for diversity and humanitarian values.

---

3. Misinformation

The spread of false or biased information exacerbates distrust and reinforces ideological echo chambers.

Example:
Social media algorithms often amplify divisive content, creating feedback loops that entrench opposing viewpoints and fuel hostility.

The Consequences of Polarization

1. Erosion of Trust

Polarization undermines trust in institutions, leaders, and even fellow citizens.

Example:
Political gridlock in the U.S. Congress has eroded public confidence in governance, as ideological divisions stall progress on critical issues.

---

2. Stagnation

Divisions hinder collaborative problem-solving, delaying action on pressing global challenges like climate change, public health, and economic reform.

Example:
International climate negotiations are often hindered by ideological disagreements over responsibility and resource allocation.

---

3. **Conflict**
    Extreme polarization can escalate into violence and societal breakdown.

    Example:
    The Rwandan Genocide was fueled by deep ethnic and ideological divides,
    demonstrating the devastating consequences of unchecked polarization.

Key Insight for Leaders

Polarization is not inevitable. Leaders have the power to heal divisions through ethical and
inclusive practices that prioritize dialogue, empathy, and shared accountability.

Strategies for Ethical Leadership in a Polarized World

To lead ethically in a divided world, leaders must actively work to bridge divides, build trust,
and promote collaboration. The following strategies provide actionable steps for addressing
polarization:

1. Foster Inclusive Dialogue

Inclusive dialogue creates platforms for open, respectful communication between opposing
groups. It allows stakeholders to share perspectives, identify common ground, and develop
solutions collaboratively.

Example: South Africa's Truth and Reconciliation Commission

Following apartheid, South Africa's Truth and Reconciliation Commission provided a space for
victims and perpetrators to share their experiences. This process fostered understanding,
accountability, and healing, demonstrating the power of dialogue in overcoming division.

Practical Steps:

- Organize town halls, forums, or digital platforms for dialogue.
- Encourage active listening, focusing on shared values and mutual goals.
- Include neutral facilitators to mediate discussions and ensure fairness.

2. Build Bridges Across Divides

Leaders must act as mediators, finding common ground between polarized groups and fostering collaboration.

Example: King Abdullah II of Jordan

As a vocal advocate for interfaith dialogue, King Abdullah II has worked to promote harmony in a region marked by religious conflict, emphasizing shared values and mutual respect.

Practical Steps:

- Identify shared interests or mutual benefits that can unite opposing parties.
- Use bridge-building initiatives, such as cultural exchange programs or joint projects, to foster cooperation.

3. Promote Shared Accountability

Ethical leaders emphasize that all parties must uphold high standards of behavior and contribute to collective solutions. Accountability ensures fairness and fosters trust.

Example: Germany's Post-War Reconstruction

After World War II, Germany's reconstruction emphasized collective accountability, rebuilding trust and stability through transparent policies and shared responsibilities.

Practical Steps:

- Develop clear guidelines for accountability and ethical behavior.
- Apply consequences for unethical actions equally, regardless of status or affiliation.

4. Lead by Example

Leaders must model the behavior they expect from others. By demonstrating ethical decision-making and integrity, they inspire others to follow suit.

Example: Jacinda Ardern's Leadership

Following the Christchurch mosque shootings, New Zealand Prime Minister Jacinda Ardern's compassionate response set a global example of ethical leadership. Her actions reflected empathy, inclusivity, and a commitment to justice.

Practical Steps:

- Make decisions transparently, explaining the ethical reasoning behind them.
- Admit and address mistakes openly, showing accountability and a commitment to improvement.

Case Study: The Good Friday Agreement

The Good Friday Agreement (1998) brought peace to Northern Ireland after decades of conflict. Its success demonstrates the transformative power of ethical leadership in resolving deep-seated divisions:

1. **Inclusivity**: The agreement included all major political parties and communities, ensuring that every voice was heard.
2. **Empathy**: Leaders acknowledged the pain and grievances of all sides, fostering mutual understanding.
3. **Compromise**: Each group made concessions for the sake of peace, demonstrating a willingness to prioritize the collective good over individual interests.

Key Insight:
Ethical leadership, rooted in empathy and inclusivity, can transform even the most entrenched divisions into opportunities for reconciliation.

The Role of Technology in Ethical Leadership

Technology is both a challenge and an opportunity in a polarized world. Ethical leaders must leverage technology to bridge divides and promote transparency, while mitigating its potential to deepen polarization.

Applications of Technology

1. **Social Media Campaigns**
   Use social media platforms to promote unity, shared values, and positive narratives.

Example:
Finland's government combats misinformation with educational campaigns on digital literacy, empowering citizens to critically evaluate online content.

2. **AI for Inclusivity**
   Employ artificial intelligence to identify and address systemic biases in governance or resource allocation.

   Example:
   AI-powered healthcare systems can ensure equitable access to resources, reducing disparities.

3. **Transparency Through Digital Platforms**
   Share data and decisions publicly to foster trust and accountability.

   Example:
   Estonia's e-governance system provides citizens with real-time access to government activities, enhancing transparency and engagement.

Reflections for Leaders

To assess your approach to ethical leadership in a polarized world, consider the following questions:

1. **Are my decisions guided by integrity, transparency, and empathy?**
2. **Have I created opportunities for dialogue and collaboration between divided groups?**
3. **Am I holding myself and others accountable to ethical standards?**
4. **Am I leveraging technology responsibly to promote unity and trust?**

Conclusion: Bridging Divides with Ethics

Ethical leadership is the antidote to polarization. By prioritizing integrity, inclusivity, and accountability, leaders can build bridges across divides, fostering trust, collaboration, and progress. In a polarized world, the most courageous leaders are those who choose empathy over exclusion, dialogue over division, and unity over conflict.

The lesson is clear: ethical leadership is not just a moral imperative but a practical strategy for building resilient and harmonious societies. Leaders who embody these principles will leave legacies of peace, progress, and unity, demonstrating that even in the face of division, the bonds of humanity are stronger than the forces that seek to tear us apart.

Chapter 9: Transforming Ideas into Movements

"Ideas spark change, but movements sustain it."

An idea, no matter how brilliant, remains a mere concept without action to bring it to life. Transforming ideas into movements is the cornerstone of impactful leadership. Movements mobilize people, inspire collective effort, and drive systemic change, turning abstract visions into concrete realities. Leaders who bridge the gap between vision and execution have the power to redefine societies, solve critical challenges, and leave enduring legacies.

This chapter explores the anatomy of movements, the leadership skills required to create them, and the strategies necessary to turn transformative ideas into sustained action.

The Power of Movements

Movements represent the collective force of individuals united by a shared vision and driven by a common purpose. They are far more than a series of isolated actions; they embody the power of community, purpose, and resilience. At their core, movements are about transforming ideas into collective action, harnessing the diverse strengths of individuals to achieve meaningful and enduring change. Successful movements transcend the contributions of individuals, channeling collective energy to address societal challenges and inspire transformation on a large scale. The strength of a movement lies in its ability to resonate with people's values, mobilize communities, and sustain momentum over time. Movements create a sense of shared purpose and foster a belief that change is not only possible but inevitable. They ignite passion, channel discontent into productive action, and serve as catalysts for progress in the face of systemic resistance.

Movements have the power to redefine norms, challenge unjust structures, and create lasting legacies. Whether addressing civil rights, environmental sustainability, or social justice, movements are essential engines of societal evolution.

The Elements of a Movement

1. A Compelling Idea

Every movement begins with a powerful idea that strikes a chord with people's values, needs, or aspirations. This idea must be clear, relevant, and inspiring, serving as the foundation for collective action. Compelling ideas often arise from a shared sense of injustice, a desire for improvement, or a vision of a better future. The power of an idea lies in its ability to galvanize individuals, offering them a sense of purpose and direction.

2. Leadership and Organization

Effective leadership is the backbone of any successful movement. Leaders provide direction, strategy, and structure, ensuring that efforts are coordinated and goals remain clear. Beyond strategy, leaders must also build trust, inspire confidence, and foster unity among participants.

Leadership is not about control but about empowering others to take ownership of the cause. Organized movements with strong leadership are better equipped to sustain momentum and navigate challenges.

3. Grassroots Participation

Movements thrive on grassroots engagement, where individuals are empowered to actively participate and contribute. Grassroots participation fosters a sense of shared responsibility and agency, making the movement feel inclusive and democratic. When people see themselves as co-creators of change, they are more likely to remain committed and inspire others to join. The collective action of individuals at the grassroots level amplifies the reach and impact of a movement.

4. Momentum and Adaptability

Sustained progress requires maintaining momentum, which involves continuous engagement, the celebration of milestones, and the ability to adapt to changing circumstances. Movements must be flexible enough to evolve in response to new challenges, opposition, or opportunities. Adaptability ensures that a movement remains relevant and resilient, capable of weathering setbacks and seizing moments of potential growth.

Historical Examples of Transformative Movements

The Civil Rights Movement

The Civil Rights Movement in the United States exemplifies the power of a movement rooted in a compelling idea—racial equality. Faced with systemic segregation and discrimination, the movement unified diverse groups to challenge institutionalized racism. Under the leadership of figures like Martin Luther King Jr., the movement employed nonviolent resistance, legal action, and public advocacy to inspire millions. Key milestones, such as the Montgomery Bus Boycott and the March on Washington, highlighted the collective strength of the movement. Legislative victories, including the Civil Rights Act of 1964 and the Voting Rights Act of 1965, cemented its legacy as a transformative force in American history.

The Green Movement

The global Green Movement, focused on environmental sustainability, has redefined how nations and societies approach issues such as climate change, renewable energy, and conservation. Sparked by growing awareness of environmental degradation, the movement galvanized grassroots activism and policy advocacy to address pressing ecological challenges. International agreements like the Paris Accord reflect the movement's ability to influence global cooperation. By emphasizing renewable energy, conservation, and sustainable practices, the Green Movement has driven significant progress toward a more sustainable future, inspiring both local and global action.

Women's Suffrage Movement

The Women's Suffrage Movement, which spanned decades, fought for women's right to vote and participate fully in democratic societies. Rooted in the idea of gender equality, the movement employed marches, petitions, legal challenges, and civil disobedience to challenge patriarchal norms. Leaders like Susan B. Anthony and Emmeline Pankhurst mobilized millions, creating a global movement that reshaped societal attitudes toward women's rights. The eventual success of the movement, marked by milestones such as the 19th Amendment in the United States, highlighted the enduring power of collective action for social justice.

Key Insight for Leaders
Movements succeed when they align with universal values, address pressing societal issues, and offer tangible solutions. They must speak to the aspirations and emotions of individuals while providing a roadmap for collective action.

1. **Craft a Clear Vision**
   A compelling and easily understood vision ensures that participants and supporters can rally around a common cause. Leaders must communicate this vision effectively, emphasizing its relevance and urgency.
2. **Foster Inclusion and Collaboration**
   Inclusive movements that welcome diverse perspectives and contributions are more likely to succeed. Collaboration strengthens the movement's foundation, ensuring it resonates with a broad audience.
3. **Maintain Resilience and Adaptability**
   Effective movements remain resilient in the face of challenges and adaptable to evolving circumstances. Leaders must anticipate obstacles and navigate them without losing sight of the ultimate goal.

By understanding the elements of a movement and learning from historical examples, leaders can harness the collective power of communities to drive meaningful and lasting change. Movements are a testament to what is possible when individuals unite around shared values and a common purpose, proving that even the most entrenched systems can be transformed through collective action.

Leadership in Action: Turning Ideas into Movements

Leadership is the linchpin of any successful movement. Leaders must not only envision change but also inspire others to believe in and work toward that vision. They play a critical role in articulating the idea, mobilizing support, and sustaining momentum.

1. Articulate a Clear Vision

Movements begin with a vision that captures the imagination of the audience. This vision must be compelling, easily understood, and deeply resonant. Leaders must communicate their vision with clarity and passion to rally support.

Example: Mahatma Gandhi

Mahatma Gandhi's vision of nonviolent resistance, or *Satyagraha*, became the cornerstone of India's struggle for independence. His ability to articulate this vision inspired millions to join the movement, turning a colonial struggle into a global symbol of justice and freedom.

Practical Steps:

- Clearly define the movement's purpose, goals, and desired outcomes.
- Use storytelling to connect emotionally with the audience and make the vision relatable.
- Highlight the urgency and relevance of the movement to inspire immediate action.

---

2. Mobilize Public Support

Building a movement requires engaging diverse stakeholders and creating a sense of shared ownership. Leaders must reach out to individuals, communities, and institutions to build a broad base of support.

Example: Greta Thunberg and Fridays for Future

Greta Thunberg's Fridays for Future campaign mobilized millions of young people worldwide to demand climate action. By appealing to universal concerns about the future, the movement gained global traction and forced leaders to confront the climate crisis.

Practical Steps:

- Leverage social media and digital platforms to amplify the movement's message and reach broader audiences.
- Organize events, protests, or campaigns to raise awareness and encourage active participation.
- Engage with diverse communities to ensure inclusivity and build a coalition of supporters.

---

3. Build Strong Networks

Movements thrive on collaboration. Leaders must establish alliances with individuals, organizations, and institutions that share their vision. These networks provide resources, expertise, and credibility, enhancing the movement's impact.

Example: The Black Lives Matter Movement

The Black Lives Matter movement grew into a global force through partnerships with local activists, nonprofits, and influencers. These alliances amplified the movement's message, mobilized resources, and sustained its momentum.

Practical Steps:

- Identify potential allies and establish partnerships based on shared goals and values.
- Foster open communication, mutual respect, and trust within the network.
- Coordinate efforts across organizations to maximize reach and impact.

4. Sustain Momentum

Movements often face periods of stagnation or resistance. Leaders must find ways to maintain energy, enthusiasm, and focus over time, ensuring that participants remain committed to the cause.

Example: The Feminist Movement

The feminist movement has sustained momentum over decades by adapting its goals and strategies to address evolving challenges, such as workplace equality, reproductive rights, and intersectionality.

Practical Steps:

- Celebrate milestones and successes to maintain enthusiasm and reinforce a sense of progress.
- Regularly update participants on the movement's achievements and future plans.
- Adapt strategies to respond to new challenges, opportunities, or societal shifts.

The Role of Technology in Movements

Technology has revolutionized how movements are organized, communicated, and amplified. Leaders must harness its potential while being mindful of its risks and limitations.

1. Social Media

Social media platforms like Twitter, Facebook, and Instagram allow movements to reach global audiences instantly, amplify voices, and engage supporters in real time.

Example: The #MeToo Movement

The #MeToo movement used social media to expose the prevalence of sexual harassment and empower survivors to share their stories. The hashtag became a rallying cry for change, influencing policies and societal attitudes worldwide.

---

2. Crowdsourcing

Technology enables movements to raise funds, gather ideas, and mobilize resources quickly and efficiently.

Example: Kickstarter and Grassroots Campaigns

Crowdsourcing platforms like Kickstarter have helped fund grassroots initiatives, from community projects to social justice campaigns, demonstrating the power of collective financial support.

---

3. Data Analytics

Analyzing data allows leaders to understand their audience, measure the impact of their efforts, and refine strategies for greater effectiveness.

Example: Political Campaigns

Modern political campaigns increasingly use data analytics to target messaging, mobilize voters, and track engagement, ensuring their resources are used strategically.

Key Insight

Technology is a tool, not a solution. Leaders must use it strategically, ensuring it aligns with the movement's goals, values, and ethical standards.

Challenges in Building Movements

Despite their potential, movements face significant challenges. Leaders must anticipate and address these obstacles to ensure their success.

1. Fragmentation

As movements grow, differing priorities, strategies, or visions can create divisions among participants.

Solution:
Establish clear goals and core values that unify the movement and provide a common direction.

2. Resistance

Movements that challenge the status quo often face opposition from powerful interests, including governments, corporations, or entrenched social norms.

Solution:
Build resilience through alliances, legal protections, and widespread public support to counter resistance effectively.

3. Burnout

Sustained activism can lead to exhaustion among participants, diminishing the movement's energy and effectiveness.

Solution:
Promote self-care and mental health support within the movement. Distribute leadership responsibilities to prevent individuals from becoming overburdened.

Case Study: The Women's Suffrage Movement

The women's suffrage movement, spanning over a century, is a powerful example of how to transform an idea into lasting change. Its success stemmed from several key factors:

1. **Vision**: The idea that women deserved the right to vote challenged entrenched norms and inspired a global call for equality.
2. **Leadership**: Figures like Emmeline Pankhurst and Susan B. Anthony provided direction, strategy, and inspiration.
3. **Adaptation**: The movement evolved its strategies, from peaceful protests to legal battles, to address changing circumstances.
4. **Outcome**: Women secured voting rights in many countries, reshaping political and social landscapes.

Practical Framework for Leaders

To transform an idea into a movement, leaders can follow these steps:

1. **Define the Core Message**: Focus on a clear, actionable idea that resonates widely.
2. **Engage Grassroots Participation**: Empower individuals to take ownership and drive change within their communities.
3. **Leverage Partnerships**: Collaborate with organizations, media, and influencers to amplify the message.
4. **Measure and Communicate Impact**: Regularly assess progress and share successes to maintain momentum.

Reflections for Leaders

To assess your ability to build movements, consider the following questions:

- Is the vision clear and compelling enough to inspire collective action?
- Have I engaged and empowered diverse stakeholders to drive the movement?
- Am I prepared to adapt strategies as the movement evolves?
- Are there mechanisms in place to sustain momentum and prevent burnout?

Conclusion: Movements as Engines of Change

Movements are the bridge between vision and reality. They transform ideas into action, mobilize communities, and reshape societies. Leaders who master the art of movement-building can address critical challenges, inspire collective effort, and leave lasting legacies.

The lesson is clear: an idea alone cannot change the world, but a movement, fueled by passion, strategy, and resilience, can. Leaders must embrace this challenge, harnessing the power of movements to drive progress and create a brighter, more equitable future.

Chapter 10: Leaving a Legacy – Leadership That Endures

"The true measure of leadership is the legacy it leaves behind."

Leadership is not confined to the successes of the present—it is about shaping a future where others can thrive. A leader's legacy is the enduring imprint of their vision, decisions, and actions. It is a testament to the values they upheld, the progress they inspired, and the systems they established. True leadership is not about transient achievements but about creating lasting impact, ensuring the well-being of future generations.

This chapter explores the principles of legacy-building, the qualities that define enduring leadership, and strategies for ensuring that a leader's influence lasts well beyond their tenure.

The Meaning of Legacy

A legacy is far more than the memory of a leader's time in power or the titles and accolades they amass. It encompasses the enduring contributions, both tangible and intangible, that continue to influence individuals, institutions, and societies long after a leader has stepped down. A legacy reflects not only what was achieved during a leader's tenure but also the values and systems they cultivated to sustain progress for future generations.

At its core, a legacy is about creating something greater than oneself—something that withstands the test of time. It is the imprint of a leader's vision, decisions, and actions, seen in the lives of those they served and the systems they shaped. A meaningful legacy fosters positive change, inspires future leaders, and lays the foundation for continued growth and development. It is the bridge between the past, present, and future, connecting generations through shared values and progress.

Leaders who prioritize their legacy focus on building systems and fostering cultures that endure beyond their immediate influence. They understand that true leadership is about empowering others, creating sustainable solutions, and leaving a world better than they found it.

Components of a Legacy

1. Vision

A compelling vision is the cornerstone of any enduring legacy. This vision defines the direction of progress, serving as a guiding light for current actions and a blueprint for future generations.

A clear and inspiring vision resonates with people's aspirations, providing them with a sense of purpose and hope.

Great leaders craft visions that are forward-thinking, inclusive, and actionable. They articulate goals that address immediate needs while anticipating future challenges, ensuring that their vision remains relevant over time. This vision becomes a touchstone for decision-making, shaping policies, initiatives, and strategies that leave a lasting impact.

2. Impact

Impact is the measurable and meaningful change that a leader brings to the lives of individuals and the systems that support them. A lasting legacy is built on tangible improvements—such as enhanced education, healthcare, infrastructure, or economic opportunities—that reflect a leader's dedication to creating a better world.

Impact is not limited to large-scale achievements; it can also be seen in smaller, transformative moments that ripple through communities and institutions. The true measure of impact lies in its ability to endure, creating systems and solutions that continue to benefit people long after the leader's direct involvement has ended.

3. Values

Ethical principles and moral standards form the foundation of a legacy that inspires and guides future leaders. A legacy grounded in strong values fosters trust, accountability, and integrity, ensuring that decisions are made with the greater good in mind.

Values provide a moral compass, shaping the culture of organizations and societies. Leaders who prioritize honesty, equity, compassion, and justice leave behind not just policies but also a framework for ethical decision-making. These values serve as a touchstone for navigating future challenges, ensuring that the leader's influence continues to promote fairness and humanity.

The Evolution of Legacy

The concept of legacy evolves over time, shaped by how future generations interpret and build upon a leader's contributions. A strong legacy is adaptable, able to withstand the scrutiny of changing social, political, and cultural contexts. Leaders who embrace innovation and inclusivity are more likely to leave legacies that resonate with diverse audiences and endure through shifts in societal priorities.

A legacy also depends on how well a leader empowers others to carry their vision forward. By fostering mentorship, collaboration, and shared responsibility, leaders ensure that their work is not confined to their tenure but becomes a continuous source of progress and inspiration.

Key Insight for Leaders

A legacy is not built overnight; it is the cumulative result of consistent, principled action. Leaders must align their daily decisions with their long-term vision to create an enduring impact. Every policy, initiative, and interaction contributes to the larger narrative of a leader's legacy.

1. **Consistency in Action**
   Legacy is shaped by the consistency of a leader's actions over time. Small, deliberate steps that align with a clear vision can build momentum and lead to transformative change.
2. **Empowering Others**
   A great legacy is not about the leader alone—it is about the people and systems they empower. By cultivating leadership in others and fostering collaborative environments, leaders ensure their vision and values endure.
3. **Focus on Sustainability**
   Leaders who prioritize sustainable solutions leave behind systems that continue to thrive without their direct involvement. Sustainability ensures that progress is not just a fleeting achievement but a lasting contribution to future generations.

Ultimately, a legacy is not measured solely by the accolades or monuments left behind but by the lives touched, the progress achieved, and the values instilled. Leaders who focus on creating meaningful and lasting change ensure that their impact will resonate far beyond their time in power, shaping a brighter and more equitable future.

Historical Legacies of Enduring Leadership

History is replete with examples of leaders whose legacies have stood the test of time. These leaders not only achieved success during their tenure but also laid the groundwork for future progress.

---

1. Nelson Mandela

Nelson Mandela's legacy is one of reconciliation, justice, and unity. After enduring decades of imprisonment, he emerged as a symbol of forgiveness and hope, leading South Africa through its transition from apartheid to democracy. His focus on building institutions, fostering inclusivity, and promoting human rights ensured that his influence extended far beyond his presidency.

---

2. Franklin D. Roosevelt

Franklin D. Roosevelt's New Deal redefined the role of government in economic recovery and social welfare. Programs such as Social Security, introduced during his presidency, remain cornerstones of American society, exemplifying how policies can create enduring social safety nets.

3. Mahatma Gandhi

Gandhi's principles of nonviolence and self-reliance inspired movements worldwide, from civil rights campaigns in the United States to anti-colonial struggles in Africa. His emphasis on ethical leadership and grassroots empowerment created a legacy that transcends borders and generations.

Key Lesson

Enduring legacies are rooted in values and actions that address universal human needs. Leaders who focus on building systems and empowering people ensure their influence lasts far beyond their lifetimes.

The Qualities of Legacy-Building Leadership

Leaders who leave lasting legacies share common qualities that guide their approach to governance and decision-making.

1. Visionary Thinking

Legacy-building leaders articulate a clear and transformative vision that inspires others. They challenge the status quo, set ambitious goals, and provide a roadmap for achieving them.

Example:
John F. Kennedy's vision of landing a man on the moon united a nation in pursuit of innovation and progress, leaving a legacy of scientific advancement and national pride.

2. Ethical Integrity

Integrity is the foundation of a lasting legacy. Ethical leaders act with honesty, fairness, and a commitment to doing what is right, even in the face of opposition.

Example:
Jacinda Ardern's compassionate leadership during crises, including the Christchurch mosque shootings, set a global standard for empathy, transparency, and ethical decision-making.

---

3. Resilience

Legacy-building leaders persevere through challenges and setbacks. They demonstrate courage in the face of adversity and use crises as opportunities for growth and innovation.

Example:
Winston Churchill's leadership during World War II showcased resilience, determination, and the ability to inspire hope during one of history's darkest periods.

---

4. Empowerment

Empowering others is a hallmark of enduring leadership. Leaders who invest in people and foster collaboration create a culture of growth and innovation that continues long after they have stepped down.

Example:
Angela Merkel's emphasis on empowering women in leadership has had a lasting impact on gender equality in politics and governance.

Building a Legacy Through Systems and Institutions

A leader's true legacy lies in the systems and institutions they create. These structures ensure continuity and resilience, enabling societies to thrive long after the leader's departure.

---

1. Strengthening Institutions

Robust, transparent institutions uphold justice, equity, and accountability. They provide the framework for governance, ensuring stability and progress.

Example:
Singapore's transformation under Lee Kuan Yew was driven by strong institutions that promoted economic stability, social harmony, and good governance.

2. Investing in Education

Education empowers future generations to solve problems, innovate, and lead effectively. It is one of the most powerful tools for creating an enduring legacy.

Example:
Finland's investment in equitable and innovative education has made it a global model of success, fostering a highly skilled and resilient population.

3. Promoting Sustainability

Policies that protect the environment and manage resources responsibly create a legacy of resilience and abundance for future generations.

Example:
Costa Rica's commitment to renewable energy and conservation has secured its reputation as a leader in sustainability, ensuring long-term prosperity for its people and ecosystems.

The Role of Reflection in Legacy-Building

Building a legacy requires intentionality and self-awareness. Leaders must continuously reflect on their actions, ensuring they align with their vision and values.

Questions for Reflection

1. **Am I prioritizing long-term impact over short-term gains?**
   Leaders must balance immediate needs with the sustainability of their decisions.
2. **Are my actions aligned with the values I want to represent?**
   Consistency between values and actions builds trust and credibility.
3. **What systems am I creating to ensure continuity after my tenure?**
   Leaders should focus on institutionalizing progress to safeguard their legacy.

Key Insight for Leaders

Reflection ensures that daily decisions contribute to the legacy a leader wishes to leave. It fosters clarity, alignment, and purpose in leadership.

Challenges in Building a Legacy

Building an enduring legacy is not without challenges. Leaders must navigate obstacles that threaten to undermine their vision and impact.

1. Resistance to Change

Established norms and vested interests often resist transformative leadership.

Solution:
Build coalitions, communicate the benefits of change, and engage stakeholders to gain support and overcome opposition.

2. Unforeseen Crises

Unexpected events, such as economic downturns or natural disasters, can derail progress and shift priorities.

Solution:
Remain adaptable, using crises as opportunities to demonstrate resilience and innovation.

3. Succession Planning

A lack of preparation for leadership transitions can jeopardize continuity and stability.

Solution:
Develop future leaders who share the vision and values of the organization, ensuring a seamless transfer of leadership.

Case Study: Barack Obama's Legacy

Barack Obama's presidency illustrates the complexities of legacy-building. His achievements and challenges provide valuable lessons for leaders:

Achievements

1. **Healthcare Reform**
   The Affordable Care Act expanded access to healthcare for millions of Americans, addressing a critical societal need.
2. **Environmental Action**
   Obama advanced climate initiatives, including the Paris Agreement, setting a global example for environmental responsibility.
3. **Leadership Style**
   His focus on inclusivity, diplomacy, and collaboration set a tone for ethical leadership and global cooperation.

Challenges

Some of Obama's policies faced backlash or reversal after his tenure, highlighting the importance of institutionalizing change to ensure durability.

Key Lesson

Leaders must focus on creating systems and policies that can withstand political shifts and challenges, ensuring their impact endures beyond their tenure.

Practical Strategies for Building a Legacy

To leave an enduring legacy, leaders can adopt the following strategies:

1. Focus on Core Values

Let principles guide every decision, creating a consistent and inspiring narrative.

2. Engage Stakeholders

Collaborate with diverse groups to ensure broad support and shared ownership of the vision.

3. Document and Communicate

Record achievements, lessons, and values to inspire future leaders and preserve the legacy.

4. Prepare Successors

Mentor and empower future leaders to carry forward the vision, ensuring continuity and resilience.

Reflections for Leaders

To evaluate the legacy you are building, consider the following:

- **What values define my leadership, and are they evident in my actions?**
- **How will my decisions impact future generations?**
- **Have I created systems that ensure continuity and resilience beyond my tenure?**

Conclusion: The Gift of a Legacy

A legacy is not about monuments or accolades—it is about the lives transformed and the systems strengthened under a leader's guidance. Leaders who prioritize integrity, vision, and sustainability leave behind a foundation for future generations to build upon. To maintain justice, no leader is above scrutiny. Moses, in the Torah, appointed judges to share the burden of governance (Exodus 18:21), which reflects the necessity of delegation and collective decision-making in modern societies. By incorporating various perspectives, societies avoid the pitfalls of centralized or unchecked authority. This framework aligns with the New Testament's teaching in Romans 13:1–7, emphasizing that rulers are servants of God for the people's good.

A leader's inability to meet their divine and moral obligations not only leads to personal failure but also societal collapse. Hence, Abrahamic scriptures collectively advocate for transparent leadership, where decisions are grounded in collective welfare and the moral compass provided by faith.

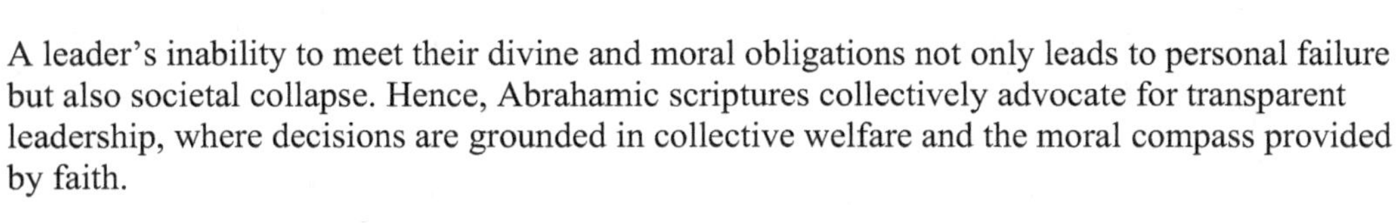

The Lesson Is Clear

Leadership is not measured by the power you wield but by the legacy you leave. Leaders who embrace this challenge create ripples that extend far beyond their time, shaping a future of equity, progress, and hope. True legacy-building is a gift to humanity, ensuring that the leader's impact endures, inspires, and empowers for generations to come.